MICRO HABITS

Also available

High Performance
High Performance: The Daily Journal
How to Change Your Life

MICRO HABITS

Tiny Changes that Supercharge High Performance

Jake Humphrey
Damian Hughes

Cornerstone Press

CORNERSTONE PRESS

UK | USA | Canada | Ireland | Australia
India | New Zealand | South Africa

Cornerstone Press is part of the Penguin Random House group of companies whose addresses can be found at global.penguinrandomhouse.com

Penguin Random House UK,
One Embassy Gardens, 8 Viaduct Gardens, London SW11 7BW

penguin.co.uk

First published 2026
005

Copyright © High Performance Life Ltd, 2026

The moral right of the authors has been asserted

Penguin Random House values and supports copyright. Copyright fuels creativity, encourages diverse voices, promotes freedom of expression and supports a vibrant culture. Thank you for purchasing an authorised edition of this book and for respecting intellectual property laws by not reproducing, scanning or distributing any part of it by any means without permission. You are supporting authors and enabling Penguin Random House to continue to publish books for everyone. No part of this book may be used or reproduced in any manner for the purpose of training artificial intelligence technologies or systems. In accordance with Article 4(3) of the DSM Directive 2019/790, Penguin Random House expressly reserves this work from the text and data mining exception.

Set in 11.25/16.7pt Sabon LT Std
Typeset by Six Red Marbles UK, Thetford, Norfolk

Printed and bound in Great Britain by Clays Ltd, Elcograf S.p.A.

The authorised representative in the EEA is Penguin Random House Ireland, Morrison Chambers, 32 Nassau Street, Dublin D02 YH68

A CIP catalogue record for this book is available from the British Library

ISBN: 978–1–529–97620–5

Penguin Random House is committed to a sustainable future for our business, our readers and our planet. This book is made from Forest Stewardship Council® certified paper.

To everyone who has shared their stories with us,
and to you – the reader – for choosing to start your own.
This book belongs as much to you as it does to us.

CONTENTS

Introduction: Small, Simple, Speedy ... 1

1: HOW TO MOTIVATE YOURSELF

Lando Norris: Job, Career or Calling? ... 15
Adam Peaty: The Odysseus Contract ... 20
Keely Hodgkinson: Motivation Hacking ... 26
Matthew McConaughey: Delayed Gratification ... 34

2: HOW TO FIND YOUR PURPOSE

Johann Hari: The Cambodian Cow ... 41
Dame Stephanie Shirley: The Bedtime Question Worth Asking ... 45
Ali Abdaal: Write Your Own Obituary ... 49
Simon Sinek: The Best-Friend Test ... 53

3: HOW TO FOCUS ON WHAT MATTERS

Will Guidara: Sweating the Small Stuff ... 59
Stuart Broad: Are You Playing to Win? ... 64
Brian Cox: Focus On What You Don't Know ... 70
Barry Hearn: What Story Are You Telling Yourself? ... 74

CONTENTS

4: HOW TO ORGANISE YOUR TIME (AND YOUR LIFE)

Shane Parrish: Show Me Your Calendar — 81
Usain Bolt: Transform Your Mindset — 85
Tom Daley: Process Goals Beat Outcome Goals — 92
Sabrina Cohen-Hatton: Three Questions for Better Decisions — 97

5: HOW TO CONNECT WITH OTHERS

Charles Duhigg: Hug, Hear or Help? — 103
AJ Tracey: The Power of Your Inner Circle — 107
George Russell: Ask for Help — 111
Dan Carter: How to Read Emotions — 115

6: HOW TO GET THE BEST OUT OF PEOPLE

Marcus Wareing: Surround Yourself with the Best — 123
Sir Ian McGeechan: Always Shout Your Round — 126
Kevin Sinfield: The Helping Hand — 130
Martin Lewis: Trust Comes First — 134

7: HOW TO BUILD A CLOSE-KNIT TEAM

Andy Cole: 'We' Not 'Me' — 141
Chris Voss: Small Talk Gets Big Wins — 145

CONTENTS

Joe Marler: Emotional Glue — 149
Pippa Grange: The Triple H — 153

8: HOW TO GIVE (AND RECEIVE) BETTER FEEDBACK

Sara Davies: Radical Candour — 159
Jordan Henderson: Dealing with Dissenters — 164
Gordon Ramsay: Don't Take It So Personally — 168
Dame Laura Kenny: Disagree Agreeably — 171

9: HOW TO PERFORM UNDER PRESSURE

Steve Peters: 'What If . . . ?' — 177
Fernando Alonso: Game Face — 182
Alex Honnold: Embrace the Fear — 185
Graham Potter: No Comfort Zones — 189

10: HOW TO DO THE WORK

Maro Itoje: The Shit People Don't See — 195
James Milner: The Commitment Principle — 199
Alun Wyn Jones: The IKEA Effect — 203
Steven Gerrard: All In — 208

11: HOW TO REST

Joe Wicks: Retire Every Year — 213
Vicky Pattison: Number Your Days — 217

Eddie Howe: Reflect to Reconnect — 221
Emily Maitlis: Golden Time — 226

12: HOW TO STAY OPTIMISTIC

James Timpson: Celebrate the Good News First — 231
Sarina Wiegman: Attitude: Gratitude — 234
Sara Pascoe: Unconditional Positive Regard — 237
Jason Fox: What Would a Commando Do? — 242

Epilogue: The Twelve-Month Micro-Habits Plan — 247

Acknowledgements — 253
Notes — 257
Index — 281
About the Authors — 289

MICRO-HABITS

MICRO-HABITS

What if you could change your life in less than five minutes?

INTRODUCTION

SMALL, SIMPLE, SPEEDY

Damian

The Australian sun was shining brightly, the blue sky was shimmering in the early morning heat, and the green grass of the rugby pitch had never looked so inviting. But the words I was hearing weren't nearly as enticing.

'We are going to start tackling practice now,' explained Tony Smith, the charismatic head coach of England Rugby League. 'Would you mind holding one of the tackle pads?'

With a gulp, I nodded my assent and trotted on to the training field. I gathered the bag, threading my arms through the straps to ensure it was held tightly.

My insides felt equally tight. Jamie Peacock, the 6ft 5in leviathan standing thirty yards away, looked like he'd been carved out of granite. As he pawed the ground, eager to commence the drill, the whole of the England camp paused their activities. Their faces were filled with an undisguised zeal at the imminent firework display, just waiting for the blue touchpaper to be lit.

Many teams have induction processes for new recruits. Over the years I have been forced to sing songs, recount bawdy encounters, even deliver a joke in front of the most hostile of audiences: your colleagues. But this was different. I had yet to experience the joy of being run into full pelt by the captain of England Rugby League. *This is my induction*, I thought, resignedly.

As Peacock began his run-up I braced for impact, planting my feet in the lush green turf and fighting the rising urge to close my eyes or run away. As he ran faster and faster I could see his steely gaze fixed firmly upon me. I braced myself: *here it comes*. I started counting down to the moment of impact: *three . . . two . . . one . . .*

Until, with his final step, the Leeds Rhinos legend subtly twisted his trunk to avoid colliding into me. The whooshing sound as he passed was matched only by the speed of the air leaving my chest. I realised I'd been unconsciously holding my breath.

I looked to the sidelines and saw the whole England team laughing. 'Thanks, Jamie,' I muttered. 'I appreciate that.'

Is it possible for a single moment to teach you everything you need to know about a team? Since arriving at England's World Cup training camp on the Gold Coast, there had been no grand welcome speeches, laminated team values or ping-pong tables in the staff areas to signal the type of culture I had entered. But Peacock's little practical joke – and the kindness in choosing to not, in fact, launch me into the Pacific Ocean – had communicated exactly what sort of team this was. Despite first appearances, I was safe here. I had been given a sense of belonging in the group. And we'd had a laugh about it too.

Throughout my career, working with teams ranging from England Rugby League to Scotland Rugby Union and England Netball, I have come to understand the power of these small and frequently overlooked occurrences. These microscopic behaviours and moments are the essential ingredient of any high-performing culture. The cement between the bricks.

Jake

I am living proof that small changes in behaviour can have an outsized impact. I transformed my life just by tweaking the time of my morning alarm.

For most of my adult life, my mornings had been a rushed blur of getting the kids to school, rushing for the train to work, all while feeling underprepared and overwhelmed. I always missed breakfast, which killed my energy. I didn't engage with my family, which killed my mojo. And I didn't get ready for the day ahead, which killed my effectiveness.

Only a couple of years ago did I do the obvious thing: I shifted my alarm clock forwards by 15 minutes. For a while, I couldn't quite believe how big an impact it had. Having just a few minutes of solitude to think about the day ahead was a revelation. By the time my wife, Harriet, and the kids woke up I was ready with cuddles and coffee. It was a small change. And it changed everything.

It was my first hint that I had been sold a myth about the path to success. For too long, high performance has been characterised as a complex, ever-changing system – one invariably tied to a pricey course or, at the very least, a bewildering 1,000-page textbook. But here's the truth: success starts simple. And it begins in moments just like when I tinkered with my morning alarm. The moments you often ignore because they seem too insignificant to matter.

I'm not the only one. Over the last five years, your two authors have completed over 400 interviews with people who have scaled the heights of their chosen professions on our podcast, *High Performance*. And we have repeatedly witnessed that a commitment to tiny, even imperceptible, behaviours of this kind makes the difference between success and failure. Every choice you make, however small, contributes to ensuring high performance and eliminating low standards. As Eddie Jones, the former England Rugby Union coach told us: 'Nothing you do is neutral.'

> **'Nothing you do is neutral.'** Eddie Jones

Sir Ian McGeechan, the legendary rugby union coach, calls these small practices with an outsized impact 'world-class basics'. He has spent his career creating cultures of sustained excellence in a succession of triumphant teams: Northampton, Wasps and, most famously, the British & Irish Lions. And he credits tiny, basic commitments for his success.[1] 'Each position or each role has certain skills that are very specific to that role,' McGeechan explained to us. 'The best are able to deliver something that can make a difference when it matters.' These small, basic skills – consistently passing the ball well, consistently being in the right position, consistently making the correct decision under pressure – all add up to elite performance.

In fact, once you start looking for these basic, consistent behaviours you start to see them everywhere. Take the words of Shaun Wane, the head coach of England Rugby League: 'How you do anything is how you do everything.' His point is that each small behaviour is a microcosm of your wider approach and values. One of his protégés, Sam Tomkins, once told us a strange story about how Shaun used to make him carry around a Filofax – a bulky, unseemly and seemingly irrelevant item most associated with *Only Fools and Horses'* Derek Trotter – everywhere he went. If he couldn't brandish it on request, the consequences would be severe. It sounded a bit weird, to be fair. But the point was simple: if Sam couldn't be trusted to do something small and specific, like carry around a Filofax, then he would never be able to do something big and expansive, like win the Super League competition.

Or take the words of Rob O'Neill, a member of the celebrated US Navy SEALs, who recounted the advice he was offered when he faced the unit's gruelling selection training – including the ordeal everyone calls 'Hell Week'. 'Here's how you get through SEAL training,' he said. 'Wake up in the morning on time, make your bed the right way and then brush your teeth. You just started your day with three wins.' These small changes changed everything. 'Because you took the time for yourself in the morning to make your bed the right way, regardless of how bad today will be – and it will be bad – tomorrow is a clean slate.'

In every case, the principle is the same. The tiny insignificant behaviours are just as important as the big obvious ones. For Ian McGeechan, it was summarised by a phrase: 'World-class basics.' For Shaun Wane, that was summarised in a mantra: 'How you do anything is how you do everything.' For Rob O'Neill, it was summarised in a few small actions such as brushing your teeth and making your bed.

We have another term for these actions. We call them micro-habits.

What are micro-habits?

'Micro-habit' is the term we have come to use for the simple, imperceptible behaviours that we have noticed many of the highest performing people depend upon. Over the years, we have come to define a micro-habit as a simple, repeatable behaviour with three qualities.

First, and most obviously, a micro-habit needs to be **small**. In our previous books we have written about big, meaty concepts – from teamwork to mindset to motivation. But in this book we want to write about how all of these big outcomes are built upon miniature strategic decisions: the little things with outsized impact. As such, nothing we suggest here will require a radical shift in your life, cost any money or require any particular skill to implement.

Second, a micro-habit needs to be **simple**. Do you remember the scene in the British sitcom, *Fawlty Towers* where the hapless hotel owner Basil Fawlty is rowing with his long-suffering wife Sybil? He suggests that should she ever participate on the quiz show, *Mastermind*, she must choose 'the bleeding obvious' as her specialist subject. Many of our high performers have a similar specialism. A lot of the ideas in this book are common sense – and that's deliberate. After all, just because an idea is simple common sense, that doesn't make it common practice.

Third, a micro-habit needs to be **speedy**. During our interviews we have been struck by the fact that many of the behaviours that the most successful people point to as being key to their success don't take very long to implement: think of Rob O'Neill brushing his teeth, or Mel Robbins high-fiving her reflection in the bathroom mirror. And that makes sense: part of what makes micro-habits successful is that you can implement them right now. That's why this book is divided into forty-eight short entries, each designed to be read quickly. Don't get us wrong: putting some of these changes into action will take a while, particularly when they amount to a major shift in mindset or perspective. But we think you can learn them – and understand them – in the time it takes to read a single entry of this book.

Our hope is that each one of these entries raises an intriguing possibility: What if you could change your life in less than five minutes? This approach might sound crazy – but in fact, the science is clear. The small details often tell you as much as the overall objectives. For example, Dr Peter Attia, one of the world's leading medical experts on how we can live longer, pointed us towards evidence showing the outsized effects that astonishingly minuscule changes in our approach to exercise can have. Undertaking just 90 seconds of vigorous physical activity per day can reduce our risk of heart attack by a third.[2] Walking 5,000 steps three times per week can add three years to their life expectancy.[3]

That is not only true for health and exercise, but for any number of your behaviours and those of the people around you. Why? Because the small changes you introduce start a chain reaction of positive actions for you, your team and your life in general. A chain reaction leads, eventually, to high performance – whatever that means to you.

In the last sentence, there was one word doing an awful lot of heavy lifting: *eventually*. This book is not offering a 'quick fix'. While these methods are quick to implement, it takes time to feel their effects.

In his book *Atomic Habits*, the psychology writer James Clear – probably the world's best-known expert on how small changes in behaviour can have outsized results – describes one fascinating study conducted by health psychologists at University College London.[4] Phillippa Lally and her colleagues monitored a number of volunteers who were seeking to incorporate one small change into their lives. Examples of these changes including eating one piece of fruit with lunch every day, another wanted to do fifty sit-ups a day. Each volunteer was then tasked with logging whether they had completed their chosen behaviour and rated the degree to which it felt habitual and whether they would find it hard *not* to complete it – a little like asking someone not to brush their teeth every morning. The idea was to explore how long it took until the participants felt the same way.

There was a significant spread among the participants' answers. Some suggested it took them just eighteen days; others, much longer. The results suggested that it took participants, on average, around sixty-six days to feel they had turned a new behaviour into a habit – that is, an effortless, automatic part of their routine.

The key takeaway is that patience matters. We all learn and change at different rates. So don't feel disappointed when things don't get easier overnight – just try your hardest to persevere.

The entrepreneur and Crystal Palace Football Club owner, Steve Parrish, captured this point when talking about a piece of advice he received from his head coach, Dougie Freedman, on our podcast. Parrish had asked whether it was appropriate to come into the dressing room after a win. His coach said it didn't matter, as long as he was also prepared to always come in after a defeat too.

The lesson: nothing is as important as consistency. 'You need to remember,' he said, 'you are only really there for the bad days.'

Small changes change everything

In the pages that follow, we have curated the most powerful micro-habits that we have come across over five years of interviews with high-performing people. They are organised into twelve domains of high performance, one for each month – and if you wish, you can apply the ideas in this book, in order, over the course of a single year. But that is not the only way to read it. You might also look through the contents page for advice on a specific challenge you're grappling with, or even just open a page at random and see what you learn.

Our promise is simple: in every chapter we will tell a story – and explain the science – behind how one small change transformed the lives of some of the most remarkable people in the world. We will show you how a simple commitment to deferring gratification helped Matthew McConaughey win an Oscar. We will delve into the small method Usain Bolt used to realise his potential, and which he credits with turning him into the fastest man in history. And we will explore how a simple commitment to expressing appreciation helped Sarina Wiegman lead the Lionesses to win the European Championship – twice.

The ideas in this book are a mixed bag, and that's deliberate. The English playwright Alan Bennett once suggested that there should be a sign placed near to the entrance of the National Gallery which reads:

YOU DON'T HAVE TO LIKE EVERYTHING IN HERE.[5]

Bennett was challenging those who passed through to be discerning rather than fawning, and active not passive, in how they saw the art. And we want this book to elicit the same response. We will share with you a wide range of examples that look at how you can kick-start your own chain reaction to high performance whether mentally or physically, personally or professionally.

Not all of them will work for you. And that's OK.

We want you to dip in and feel free to dismiss any micro-habits that are definitely not for you – and pick just a few that are.

By the end, we hope you'll have a toolkit of simple behaviours for high performance – but personalised for your own journey to success. Remember Shaun Wane's maxim: 'How you do anything is how you do everything.' But that doesn't mean that each of us has to do everything the same way. How boring would that be?

1

How to Motivate Yourself

MICRO-HABITS

Don't get a job.
Create a calling.

LANDO NORRIS

JOB, CAREER OR CALLING?

When we sat down with Lando Norris, the lead driver for Formula One team McLaren, we thought he would want to talk about his recent successes in the driver's seat that he had occupied since the age of nineteen – he was on the cusp of helping McLaren win their first Constructors' Championship since 1998, while also finishing as runner-up in the Drivers' Championship. But nothing seemed to be further from his mind.

Instead, he embarked upon an intriguing series of reminiscences about his early days in the sport when he first joined the team. When he started out, he had spent countless hours working in the garages, helping the team pack, prepare and assemble the caravan of materials needed to get the fastest possible car on to the track. 'Before I was the driver for McLaren I did some of my work experience here, just kind of getting to know everyone,' he explained. 'I would stay with the mechanics. I would pack up the garage and take the car apart after the races and stuff like that. I love everything that goes into it.'

At first we were slightly taken aback. Why did a man who was at the top of F1 want to spend all this time dwelling on his past? But eventually we came to understand: he was showing us that the things that motivated him when he started out were, on some level, the same as the things that were motivating him today.

'There was no downside,' he told us. 'There's no negative. Like, what else you gonna do? Go home and play on the Xbox in the hotel for a bit or go and grab dinner a couple hours earlier? There's no gain for me in doing that.'

> 'There was no downside. There was no negative. Like, what else you gonna do?'
> Lando Norris

Why? Because he truly, genuinely enjoyed his work in the garages – it transcended just being a job to become something dramatically more important. 'I knew there was enjoyment in it and there's the bonus of working with the team more, and our relationship is improving. I didn't know at that time that I was going to be in the racing seat a couple years later, but now it's only gonna be a good thing for me that we have that relationship and bond.'

Many of the high performers we have spoken to exhibit this kind of monomaniacal commitment to their job. Their thinking can be understood when we view it through the lens of research led by Dr Amy Wrzesniewski, a professor at Yale School of Management, who has spent much of her career researching how individuals think about their work and how this affects performance.[1]

She has found that people tend to have one of three 'work orientations' – or ways in which they think about their work. She summarises it as either a job, a career or a calling.

A job provides you with pay, benefits and perhaps a few social perks. But it is essentially about the monthly pay packet that lands in your bank account. People in this category tend to value their lives outside of the office more than their lives inside. Work is how they pay for the things they actually love: be it their friendships, hobbies or family life.

People who view their job as a career work not only out of necessity but also to advance and succeed. They tend to be more driven to seek out opportunities, strive for the next promotion and embrace training and development. People with a career orientation tend to prioritise their long-term professional future, using goals and healthy competition at work to get ahead.

Finally, those who experience their work as a calling tend to view work as an end in itself. They feel a deep emotional connection to their work, believing that it contributes to the greater good, allows them to use their strengths and gives a sense of purpose to their lives. Unsurprisingly, people with a calling orientation not only find work more rewarding, but they tend to work harder and longer because of their commitment to it – and, in turn, get better results.

Lando Norris, it seemed to us, exhibited all the hallmarks of the third approach. He wasn't just working for the sake of working. He was working because he had a deep, unwavering passion for what he was doing.

You might be thinking, *Well, good for Lando*. But not everyone can have that kind of relationship with their work. If your job is cleaning toilets then you might struggle to find a deep, unwavering passion.

But what if, in fact, you can? Wrzesniewski's findings suggest that it doesn't really matter what job you have, because a calling orientation is as much to do with your mindset as the actual work you do. The trick lies in what organisational psychologists call 'job crafting', which essentially requires you to adjust the way you think about work and reframing what you are doing so it aligns more closely with the sense of what matters to you.

In her most famous example, Wrzesniewski describes a cleaner at a hospital who defined her role not as cleaning up other people's mess or scrubbing floors but as being a 'healer' who maintained the standards in the hospital and so, in turn, contributed to the recovery of everyone inside. 'Defining her role as healer meant she paid additional attention to the tasks that might help people recover and leave the hospital more quickly,' Wrzesniewski wrote. 'She also formed relationships with patients and their families, getting to know them as people, not just temporary patients.'[2] By reframing what her work actually was, the cleaner was able to find dramatically more value in doing it.

This is quite similar to the way Lando Norris described his gruelling work in the garage. He was not just fixing the odd bit of metal, he told us. Instead, he 'got to know the values of people and how much of a difference that can make.' Even the tasks that felt the most menial were making a difference to making the car go faster.

JOB, CAREER OR CALLING?

Lando's experience shows the value that 'job crafting' can have for any of us. Think about the tasks you have to do and consider how you could rewrite them in a way that would appeal to someone who is applying for the job. What additional meaning could you find in the tasks before you if you framed them in the right terms? And what could it teach you about motivating yourself?

The overall lesson? Don't get a job. Create a calling.

WATCH
THE EPISODE

ADAM PEATY

THE ODYSSEUS CONTRACT

The first time we met Adam Peaty, he had his bags packed and his ticket ready to head to the Tokyo Olympic Games. He confidently described to us how he planned to dominate his rivals and bring gold medals back to his Derbyshire home. Weeks later, that's exactly what he did.

This series of events was entirely consistent with his whole career. Indeed, everything about Peaty's record seemed perfect: with a knack for hoovering up swimming world records and gold medals with metronomic efficiency, he once described himself as possessing a 'gladiator mindset'.

And yet just a year after our conversation, everything had changed. 'Fourteen months from that interview, I had a breakdown,' he told us in his second podcast appearance a few years later. 'This sport of swimming ... is incredibly hard.' He paused. 'Life's incredibly hard, right?'

His trouble began when he started recording strangely pedestrian times in his training. Then, as he began his preparation to become the first person to win the men's 100m breaststroke title in three Olympic Games in a row during the summer of 2024, everything went off the rails. 'I got to a place after coming off a training camp for ten weeks, [where I was] missing my son and missing home. I kept getting ill. It was my body telling me, "You don't want to do this. You can't do this."

'I went to Edinburgh to race and my times were ridiculously slow. I got back home three days later and did a warm-up, and I just felt weak ... I finished, I touched the wall and my goggles were filled with tears.' Mel Marshall, his loyal coach and mentor, was waiting by the poolside. She asked him if he was OK. 'That's the first time I've ever said no,' Peaty recalled.

Peaty described the feelings of desolation that threatened to engulf him as he stood in the shower. 'I got into the shower, just crying. Mel was there and I said, "I don't want to do this anymore."' He agreed to step away from the relentless demands of swimming for a week, which was soon extended to a second week and then a third. During this period, he began to 'question if Paris was even on the agenda.'

The solution to Adam's problem came from an unlikely source: Homer's *Odyssey*.

In Homer's ancient story, the hero Odysseus encounters the Sirens, mythical creatures with beautiful voices who lure sailors to their deaths by singing enchanting songs. To avoid this fate, Odysseus had his crew plug their ears with beeswax and tied himself to the ship's mast, allowing him to hear the Sirens' song while being prevented from steering towards them, thus successfully passing the island and escaping their deadly charm.

Today, an 'Odysseus Contract' fulfils a similar function.[1] It draws on this story's acknowledgement that we are all weak and human and often, when faced with temptation, likely to fall. If we create a constraint – the equivalent of tying ourselves to the mast – and find a way to ensure it can't later be overruled, even if we're faced with temptation or are of unsound mind, it can help us achieve our objectives without the risk of distraction.

Mel Marshall suggested that Peaty try this for himself. When he felt ready, Peaty was invited to a meeting with the head coach of Aquatics GB, where this contract idea was presented to him in the form of three simple questions: 'It was put to me: "What is it going to take to get there? Do you even want to do it? Are you willing to pay the price?"'

Knowing the price was the important question. 'You will have a receipt,' Peaty emphasised. 'When you stand up at the Olympic Games, you will have to show your receipt of hard work. If you don't, your mind will play tricks on you. *You don't deserve to be there. You haven't done the work.*' Like the Sirens calling Odysseus, Peaty knew he had to prepare by answering the questions. 'It comes back to: Do I want to do it? Am I willing to pay the price?'

'Do I want to do it? Am I willing to pay the price?' Adam Peaty

What, we wondered, was the cost? 'Everyone throws around the word "sacrifice",' he began. 'I don't believe it is a sacrifice because it's my choice to be there.' He then offered an itemised account of what the contract demanded from him should he chose to accept the deal. 'I'm covering about ten thousand metres a day plus all the gym work. That doesn't bother me. It's the time I then lose ... because you will be so broken physically and mentally that you can't even operate. You've got the time away from your family, time away from my son and seeing him grow. I feel guilty for spending that time away.

'The constant effort of human excellence is a high price,' he summarised. 'To constantly find a pathway to human excellence is probably one of the hardest things to do.'

Before he finally committed, he chose to call upon the counsel of one the greatest swimmers of all time. 'I spoke to Michael Phelps. I saw him and asked, "What did it take to bring you back?"' Phelps, who had twice retired from the sport in which he amassed an astonishing twenty-three Olympic gold medals, had a succinct response. 'He goes, "Forget all the bullshit. What does your heart tell you?"'

Eventually, Peaty was able to find his answer. 'I knew that the pain of regret would be greater than the pain of loss. It was never about medals this time. It was about taking the opportunity and not regretting the opportunity.'

The strategy worked. On a balmy Parisian night, an emotional Peaty was denied his historic treble by the narrowest of margins, coming joint second to Italy's Nicolò Martinenghi by only 0.02 seconds, less time than the blink of an eye. But he gave a tearful poolside interview where he offered millions of television viewers a small glimpse into the torments he had overcome to be there. 'It's been a very long way back ... I gave my absolute all there,' he said. 'I executed it as well as I could. It's not about the end goal, it's all about the process and it doesn't matter what the time says on the score because in my heart I've already won. I'm not crying because I've come second,' Peaty said. 'I'm crying because it took so much to get here.'

When he looked back at this raw footage, he was unequivocal. 'I gave my absolute best in that environment. I had Covid at the time when I was racing and my lungs literally couldn't work. I touched the wall and I think it was my most favourite race because of what it took to get to that moment.' He smiled as he recalled, 'My son was in the crowd, my fiancée Holly, my mum and all the people I care about. Yeah, Paris was a very good one in terms of what I expected out of myself.'

While we may not be planning to compete at an Olympic Games, the method of using a commitment contract is a powerful tool for anyone. It seems that there are three component parts to designing your own: a clear goal, a referee to hold you to account and a suitable incentive as a reward. In one analysis of over 125,000 commitment contracts, it was found that those who wrote one but failed to appoint a referee – that is, someone to hold them to account – or didn't set themselves a financial penalty succeeded only 29 per cent of the time. This rate sharply rose to 59 per cent when a referee was used and to 71.5 per cent when there was money at stake. Best of all, when a commitment contract included both a referee and financial stakes the success rate increased to nearly 80 per cent.[2]

Peaty would recognise the effectiveness of this approach and the ensuing positive results. 'A lot of people, especially in the Olympic Games, see 1 per cent of what it takes. They don't see the 99 per cent in the dark. Those dark moments are going to make or break you. Everyone in life has those moments, whether you're a seven-year-old kid wanting to go to the Olympics or a forty-year-old picking up sport again. You have to go through those moments to really define who you are, what values you are setting yourself, but also where you want to be next week or in two years' time.'

WATCH
THE EPISODE

KEELY HODGKINSON

MOTIVATION HACKING

Keely Hodgkinson wasn't always motivated by the prospect of winning Olympic medals. Once upon a time, she was motivated by getting a new pair of trainers.

The Olympic champion was on the *High Performance* podcast describing the origins of her journey to the summit of her sport. 'I was racing a girl at the Greater Manchester Schools,' Hodgkinson told us. 'You think it's the world at that age and I didn't want to do it. I was really nervous. I was just crapping myself. I didn't really know how to cope with the nerves.'

She disclosed her fears to her dad, Dean, who offered her an interesting proposal. 'I knew that me and this girl was going to be really, really close. My dad bribed me with a pair of shoes. He was like, "If you do it, I'll take you to Selfridges and get you a pair of shoes."' Keely shakes her head and smiles at the memory of his unexpected offer. 'It's probably the only time that he's ever done it. He now tells me, "I had to ring your mum and say, I'm really sorry; I had to bribe her."'

But it worked. 'I did it, and I won by 0.01 seconds,' Hodgkinson laughed. She still thinks that that 'bribe' was the starting point of her whole career. 'I'm adamant that if he hadn't have made me do that race, I think I would have just quit. He really pushed me out of my comfort zone.'

Hodgkinson's response to a material incentive – in this case, a pair of shoes – offers an intriguing insight into the science of motivation. It was a classic example of what psychologists call 'extrinsic' motivation. Essentially, extrinsic motivation refers to actions motivated by some outcome or reward – money, prestige or perhaps a new pair of trainers.

We were particularly interested in whether this type of motivation was what was driving Keely throughout her career, or whether other kinds of motivation had soon started to kick in. Our first glimpse of an answer came in her description of the next major moment in her running career. 'When I was about twelve, I had an ear operation,' she explained. 'I had a mastoidectomy, which is like a tumour that grows, and it had been growing for about ten years. It crushed all my muscles leaving me half deaf. I had to get it removed, but because it was near the brain, I literally couldn't walk, I couldn't go to school for a month and then had to have three months off any kind of activity. Even though I was so young, I was still training quite a lot.'

This enforced time out was tough for the restless teenager. 'I actually wanted to quit,' she said. Eventually, she managed to return to the track. But what she found this time round was that her motivation was completely different. At first, it was all about the pleasure of being on the track: 'I was just going to do it for fun,' she told us. And in time, another desire emerged. 'Soon my competitive side kicked in,' Keely said. 'All of a sudden, I won my first national title when I was fifteen. The next year was the European under-eighteens and I said to my dad, "I really want to make that team the next year." I ended up winning it on my international debut.'

These forms of motivation – rooted in the inherent satisfaction of doing something, or the desire to better yourself – are of a wholly different kind to that which Hodgkinson had experienced previously. It is 'intrinsic motivation', and is an altogether more powerful kind of motivation than the 'extrinsic' kind embodied by that pair of trainers.

The discovery of the two kinds of motivation originated in an experiment undertaken by two young psychologists at the University of Rochester in 1977 – one that would change our understanding of motivation.[1] Edward Deci and Richard Ryan had given two groups of psychology students a task, designed to test their problem-solving skills. Two groups of students were asked to solve three puzzles. After the second puzzle was completed, Deci and Ryan explained to both groups that they had to leave the room to get some paperwork.

They left the room and, instead of getting any papers, they spent the next eight minutes observing the group through a two-way mirror. They watched both groups spend an average of 3.5 minutes working with the puzzle pieces, trying to work them out.

On the second day, the researchers mixed it up. Group One were informed they would be rewarded with a dollar for each puzzle they got right. Group Two, unaware of this, were once again asked to complete the puzzles with no reward. Again, after puzzle two was completed, Deci and Ryan left the room for exactly eight minutes.

This time, the group who had been rewarded for completing the puzzles spent more time working on them. They seemed more motivated. On the other hand, the group who hadn't been given a reward behaved in about the same way as they had the day before. No surprises there: when you offered people a prize, they worked harder.

More surprising was what happened on the third day. This time, Deci and Ryan did something radical. Group One were told that the money had dried up: there was no financial reward for solving the puzzles. Group Two, once again, were asked to complete the task with no mention of a reward.

Group One started the task as usual – but soon it became clear something had changed. In their eight minutes of free time they spent significantly less time working on the puzzles than they had the day before, getting distracted by the magazines littered around the room rather than working on the puzzles in front of them. Whereas Group Two used the downtime to spend longer than ever working on the puzzle.

What was going on? For the group offered a cash reward, the motivation hadn't lasted. It appeared that external rewards can give a temporary boost to our motivation, but the effects quickly wear off. Those who'd been offered money no longer seemed to feel the intrinsic motivation to keep working. The group who had never been offered any money at all, however, kept their motivation up across the three days.

This study, which is today one of the most-cited studies in the history of psychology, demolished the belief that the best way to get human beings to perform tasks is to give them rewards. In time, Deci and Ryan began to develop a new model of human motivation – one they called 'self-determination theory'.[2] In short, their theory said that when motivation is driven by internal, 'self-determined' aspirations – like personal growth and self-development – it is associated with higher levels of self-esteem, and lower levels of depression and anxiety. On the other hand, placing strong relative emphasis on external aspirations – wealth and fame, for example – is associated with lower self-esteem and higher levels of depression and anxiety.

Keely Hodgkinson's experience is case in point. When she started out, she was motivated solely by the extrinsic rewards – that pair of trainers. But in time, her success became much more rooted in the intrinsic kind: the desire to beat her own records and the sheer pleasure of running.

Today, Keely attributes most of her success to the latter kind of motivation. When she competed at her first Olympics in Tokyo 2021, the exhilaration of winning a silver medal quickly gave way to a dark period where her desire to train was hard to find. With the help of her coaching team, she came to understand that she needed to discover the importance of intrinsic motivators.

'When I first went to Tokyo I was very much an underdog,' she told us. 'I look back and it was so easy. I was young, it didn't matter if I made the final or not.' But soon enough, that happy-go-lucky attitude gave way to a darker one. By the time of Paris in 2024, 'I really didn't want to be the one that got lucky and just got that medal one time. I now wanted to win on a weekly basis.'

To make this feasible, she forced herself to home in on those intrinsic pleasures – just like she had when she was starting out. 'It was about finding the pleasures in the small things. In taking it day by day. Whether that was literally getting out of bed and making your bed in the morning. I couldn't look too far ahead.' This patient, methodical approach eventually began to lift her spirits. 'I found joy in the small things and I wanted to feel like it wasn't a chore to go to training; it was a pleasurable thing.' This approach, she says, was ultimately what allowed her to train hard to win gold at Paris in 2024.

This makes sense. In the literature on the motivation spectrum, extrinsic motivation tends to be vilified and intrinsic motivation tends to be celebrated. The theory goes that the more 'intrinsic' your motivation is, the better.

But what we found most interesting about Hodgkinson's approach was the way that, in different moments, she harnessed the power of different types of motivation to succeed – even the 'bad' kind of motivation.

After all, Keely was clear: a big part of her motivation really was extrinsic – she was, as she put it, always 'racing for a medal'. And she described to us how the motivation to win gold was ultimately what drove her over the finish line in Paris. 'I really wanted to upgrade to that gold medal and it's something I've been working on with my psychologist,' she said. 'It can be quite scary thinking, "How am I going to find this extra 1 per cent?"'

She explained her way of doing this. 'I'm quite a visual

person. In Tokyo, I knew I was going to get the silver as I had visualised it all the time. I also knew I was going to run 1:55, so when it happened I wasn't necessarily surprised.'

As she reflected on the motivation behind the long hours of gruelling training, she explained that she was visualising a reward that sits firmly at the extrinsic end of the motivation spectrum. 'If I get the gold, it's a nice payday and I will buy myself a new car.' After a little prompting, she revealed exactly what type it was. 'I want a Porsche, a low-down sports one, in this really nice beige colour.' She conjured the image in her mind. 'It's just hot,' she said.

Hodgkinson's approach hints at a powerful and counter-intuitive way to think about motivation. It is not as simple as intrinsic being 'good' and extrinsic being 'bad'. While it's certainly true that extrinsic motivation tends not to work as a motivator in the long term, when you are aiming for an immediate, specific and tangible goal – literally getting to the finish line of a race, for example – it can be a powerful motivator.

Seen in this light, the trick is to home in on which type of motivation is going to work in any given situation. Are you trying to complete a big, long-term shift in who you are? In this case, you need to motivate yourself intrinsically – focusing on the deep fulfilment that you will get from changing your behaviour.

But are you simply trying to complete a gruelling, immediate, short-term task? If so, then maybe extrinsic motivation is your friend. Think of it as 'motivation-hacking': picking the type of motivation that will work for you and aligning it with your behaviour.

MOTIVATION HACKING

Hodkinson's career demonstrates that, used correctly, extrinsic motivation has its place. Would you allow yourself to buy the car if you got silver at Paris in 2024? we asked. Her answer was as quick as her running. 'No.' She was unequivocal. No gold medal, no Porsche.

WATCH
THE EPISODE

MATTHEW MCCONAUGHEY

DELAYED GRATIFICATION

'Delayed gratification, man,' Matthew McConaughey boomed from the computer screen. 'It's a tough one to teach. But boy, it's one they need to know.'

Known for his versatility and charismatic screen presence, McConaughey had just a few years previously received an Academy Award for his performance in *Dallas Buyers Club*. But the acclaimed Texan actor wasn't coming on the podcast to talk about his prize-studded acting career – he was there to talk about being a dad.

He described to us a conversation he had recently had with his son. 'Hey, you get homework on Friday? You don't have school till Monday and you got an hour of homework,' he recalled saying. 'You want to do it right now, so you can have Sunday night free?' His son's response was firm. 'No, I want to save it.'

McConaughey described how he saw this as a teaching moment. He responded, 'All right. We might be playing footy in the backyard [on] Sunday and you're going to have to leave the game.' His son was resolute. 'I'll chance it come Sunday.'

Sure enough, when Sunday rolled around he was playing football with his son. 'You gotta go do your homework,' he recalls telling him. 'Oh no. I wish I'd have done it.' 'Yeah, you would. If you'd have just nipped it in the bud Friday, you'd have had Sunday free.'

If adults think they're immune to this kind of thinking, McConaughey says, they need to stop kidding themselves. 'I'm always trying to show how far down the line can we think,' he said. 'A kid doesn't project till tomorrow, a kid doesn't even project an hour ahead, sometimes a minute ahead. As we grow up, the question is: How far can we project?

'What do you think?' he asked us. 'Next week? Next year? Five years? Ten? Can you think all the way to your eulogy?'

> 'Can you think all the way to your eulogy?'
> Matthew McConaughey

McConaughey told us how this emphasis on delayed gratification had helped him throughout his professional life. He offered us an insight into the discipline it took him to lose approximately 47 pounds for his role as Ron Woodroof in *Dallas Buyers Club*, a man dealing with a diagnosis of HIV/AIDS in the 1980s; a task which was by no means easy. 'You start and if you stick with it, the longer you stick with it, you start to get a sort of honour and pride with it.' This sense of pride was what allowed him to commit to this decision in the long term. 'I became kind of arrogant to the family,' he laughed. 'I'd be like, "oh, y'all going out to eat pizza." I was like a king on my own island ... You gotta commit to the original choice.'

But it wasn't straightforward. In the end, the results of his commitment would only pay off about eighteen months later when he won the Academy Award for Best Actor. He used the award to reinforce the lesson of delayed gratification at home. 'When I won that trophy, my kids go, "What's the trophy for?" I said, "You remember a year and a half ago when I was working and I got real skinny and you said I looked like a giraffe because my neck was so ..."' – he extended his neck. '"Remember how you'd wake up in the morning and I'd already be at work and I'd be gone all day and then get back home at night? I did the work that I was doing each day for that month and a half, my peers deemed it to be excellent and gave me a trophy for what I did a year and a half ago. They gave me a trophy for it today."'

McConaughey isn't the only one who thinks delayed gratification is important. Among scientists, whenever the term comes up you can almost guarantee that the name Walter Mischel will follow shortly. The renowned psychologist is synonymous with this concept, largely due to his famous marshmallow test.[1] In this task, young children were placed in a room with a single marshmallow placed before them and a simple choice to consider: eat the marshmallow right away or wait a little longer and have two marshmallows instead.

If you look this test up online, you'll find dozens of amusing, heart-warming and agonising videos documenting what happens next. Some kids gobble down the marshmallow right away, while the majority try to wait for the experimenter to return with the promised second sweet treat.

In Mischel's original 1972 study, the length of time in how long kids could last before giving up was hugely varied. However, when the researchers caught up with these children later in life, they discovered that those who had waited the longest had better life outcomes, including higher academic success[2] and better health.[3] Since the publication of this study, on self-control, it's been argued that those with the most perseverance and grit tend to be the most successful later in life.[4]

But when Mischel developed his test, he was less interested in measuring self-control as an end in itself and more interested in how circumstances could change children's desires to delay gratification. And, half a century after his first findings were published, what is most interesting is how *malleable* our ability to delay gratification is. In fact, the determining factor in our ability to control our urges seems less to do with nature – our genes – and more to do with culture – our surroundings.

For example, in 2022 researchers investigated the possibility that children will choose how long to wait for rewards based on what they have grown used to waiting for in their own culture.[5] In many western cultures there is not a common custom at mealtime of waiting until everyone is served before eating your food; this contrasts sharply with many eastern cultures where waiting until everyone has been served is an accepted norm. Because of this distinction, the researchers wondered whether Japanese children would take longer in the marshmallow test than American children in Mischel's original study. They tested this idea and discovered that Japanese children waited an average of fifteen minutes, while American children waited only five minutes. This is an important insight because it demonstrates that self-control is not a fixed skill – it is one that can be nurtured and developed.[6]

So, what can we all do to improve our levels of self-control? Our guests have offered a rich variety of suggestions. Some use implementation intentions, such as setting clear 'if–then' plans, like, 'If I feel the urge to check my phone, then I'll take three deep breaths first.' Others have limited their exposure to temptation by deliberately rearranging their everyday environment to reduce triggers, such as keeping snacks out of sight; while others deliberately practise short-term discomfort, such as waiting five minutes before deciding if they still want to eat a snack.

But whatever your method, the trick is being unwavering in your commitment to delay gratification – or so thinks McConaughey, anyway. He uses the example of going out to train, knowing the rewards will only come down the line. 'The hardest part about working out is putting on your damn shoes and getting out the door,' he says. 'You initially go: *this is not negotiable*. And I know it's gonna get a little wobbly and I'm gonna try to argue myself out of it. Don't listen to that voice. It's very clear. This is what we're doing.'

WATCH
THE EPISODE

2

How to Find Your Purpose

MICRO-HABITS

You can't know who you *are* until you know what you are *for*.

JOHANN HARI

THE CAMBODIAN COW

Johann Hari was telling us about the cow that cured depression.

'I interviewed a South African psychiatrist called Dr Derek Summerfield who told me what happened in Cambodia when they first introduced chemical antidepressants,' the acclaimed writer told us, enthusiastically. 'They'd never had them in that country before and the local doctor said to him, "What are antidepressants?" He'd never heard of them.'

Dr Summerfield explained to his bemused colleagues how the chemicals worked. The local doctors listened intently before suggesting that they already had a similar medicine that they sometimes dispensed to patients. 'They told him a story about a farmer in their community who worked in the rice fields. One day, he stood on a landmine left over from the war and he got his leg blown off.'

The injured farmer was fitted with a prosthetic limb and

eventually returned to work in the rice fields. But it was hard. 'It's super-painful to work underwater when you've got an artificial limb and, I'm guessing, it's also pretty traumatic to go and work in the field where you got blown up,' Hari reasoned. 'The guy soon started to cry a lot, he then refused to get out of bed and developed what we would call "classic depression".

'This is when the Cambodian doctors gave him an anti-depressant,' Hari said. 'One of the doctors thought, *If we bought this guy a cow, he could become a dairy farmer and he wouldn't be in this position that was screwing him up so much*.' Johann shifted forwards in his seat to convey his excitement about the results. 'They bought him a cow and within a couple of weeks, his crying stopped; within a month, his depression was gone and it never came back.' It gave him a renewed sense of meaning and purpose, beyond just tilling the fields every day. 'The cow was an antidepressant,' Hari concluded.

Hari, an acclaimed journalist and bestselling author, had joined the podcast to tell us about his research on depression – made famous by his bestselling book *Lost Connections*. He argues that the way we think about depression is fundamentally flawed. 'If you've been raised to think the way we have, that story sounds like a weird joke: I went to my doctor for an antidepressant, she gave me a cow,' he says. 'Yet, what those Cambodian doctors knew intuitively from this individual – and unscientific – anecdote, is what the leading medical body in the whole world, the World Health Organization, has been trying to tell us for years: if you're depressed, you're not weak, you're not crazy – you're a human being with unmet needs.'

'If you're depressed, you're not weak, you're not crazy – you're a human being with unmet needs.' Johann Hari

This is an insight that has implications well beyond the study of depression. Most of us know that as human beings we have a set of physical needs – for sustenance, shelter and clothing. But we are all too likely to overlook the psychological needs that must be met for us to be able to thrive: to belong, and to have a sense of meaning and purpose in our lives.

Across study after study, scientists have found that when humans have a sense of purpose – their very own 'Cambodian Cow' – they tend to have better outcomes than when they don't. In one classic example, Patrick Hill and colleagues at the University of Rochester Medical Center followed participants over a fourteen-year research project, in which 9 per cent of the original group passed away. From this group, it was found that a significant number of the deceased had reported having a lower purpose in life and possessing fewer positive relations than did survivors. 'Our findings point to the fact that finding a direction for life and setting overarching goals for what you want to achieve can help you actually live longer, regardless of when you find your purpose,' Hill wrote. 'So the earlier someone comes to a direction for life, the earlier these protective effects may be able to occur.'[1]

MICRO-HABITS

All this indicates that finding your own sense of purpose leads to long-lasting effects, not only on your happiness and your wealth but also your health. If you can find your own Cambodian Cow, you'll be well on your way to not only a better life but a longer one.

WATCH
THE EPISODE

DAME STEPHANIE SHIRLEY

THE BEDTIME QUESTION WORTH ASKING

The faltering step; the long pauses to catch her breath and compose herself; the rheumy eyes. All were signs that we were speaking with an eighty-nine-year-old woman. But while we had warned ourselves beforehand to be patient, in the end that wasn't necessary – Dame Stephanie Shirley spoke with all the articulacy and energy of someone decades younger. There was no chance of her letting us underestimate the person sat before us.

That's because Shirley has spent a lifetime upturning expectations and defying the odds. As we listened, she took us back through the key points of her remarkable life. Her name alone – the third she has had – offers an insight into the turbulence and challenges she has faced.

Born Vera Buchthal in Dortmund in 1934, she was just five years old when she and her older sister Renate were dispatched along with thousands of other children to board the Kindertransport train from Vienna to London to escape the dangers of imminent warfare, never knowing if they would see their parents again.

The sisters were placed with loving foster parents in the West Midlands. It was here that a moment would come and define her entire life, and, in turn, an entire industry. 'My life was saved,' she recounted. 'I was very young, but what I remember strongly is well-meaning neighbours saying to me, "Aren't you lucky to be saved?"' This simple statement had a deep impact. 'It left me with the feeling that I need to justify my own existence.'

This question – How can I make my life one worth saving? – would doubtlessly have been recognised by the famed psychoanalyst, Viktor Frankl, who once wrote that it is people's search for meaning that defines them as human beings. We all have a powerful need to make sense of our lives and find a calling that goes beyond thinking about our own basic needs. People, as Frankl put it, want to answer the questions 'Why?' and 'What for?' Put simply, you can't know who you *are* until you know what you are *for*.

Frankl believed that if they could answer these questions, individuals could bear the most horrific challenges that life could throw at them. It was something that he learned above all when, in 1942, he was taken to a concentration camp. Inside Auschwitz and, later, Dachau he found that even when lacking security, shelter and food, the creation of meaning helped people survive.

A significant part of Frankl's thinking is that meaning doesn't simply appear as a sudden revelation but rather as something that people have to continually create and work towards. This sense of meaning is founded on how people think about their activities. Frankl is fond of quoting one of his patients: 'A person who assumes that life consists of stepping from success to success is like a fool who stands next to a building site and shakes his head, because he cannot understand why people dig deep when they set out to build a cathedral.'[1]

Shirley's life offers a powerful lesson on the power of Frankl's ideas – about meaning as something that must continually be found and refound in the course of a life. In each decade of her experience, she said, she had been driven by this 'struggling to give meaning to your life, that you're not just eating and drinking, but that you actually have some meaning of the purpose that you're here.'

This desire to find meaning led her to some unexpected places. First, it led her to found a unique company. In the early 1960s, by then a British citizen and married with a new name, Shirley was finding the constant sexism that women faced in the workplace trying. So she decided to start her own company, writing software for the black box flight recorder used in Concorde and staffed by women working from home.

Despite this initial success, a woman couldn't open a bank account without her husband's permission. Her husband Derek suggested she began signing her letters using the family nickname 'Steve'. The bank account was granted before the ruse was detected and the business flourished. Dame Stephanie has been known to her friends as 'Steve' ever since. By the year 2000, Freelance Programmers – the name of the business – was valued at almost $3 billion, and over seventy of the original staff had acquired millionaire status.

Later on, this search for meaning would lead her to philanthropy. Her late son Giles was autistic and inspired her philanthropic work in the field of autism. When caring for Giles at home became impossible Shirley determined that Giles should not live his entire life in a hospital environment – leading her to found Kingwood, a residential home for autistic people, now known as Autism at Kingwood. Giles was the first resident. Ultimately it would lead her not to find meaning on her own terms but to help other people find their own. In 1996 she established the Shirley Foundation, one of the top fifty grant-giving foundations in the UK.

It has been a meaningful life by anyone's standards. When, in August 2025, Shirley died at the age of ninety-one, there was an international outpouring of grief – and universal recognition of all she had accomplished. And it reminded us of a poignant moment at the end of our conversation two years previously, when we asked how she would like to be remembered. Her answer circled back to the question she had first been posed at just five years of age. 'She was worth saving.'

WATCH
THE EPISODE

ALI ABDAAL

WRITE YOUR OWN OBITUARY

'If the thing that you are doing for work fundamentally is misaligned with what you want to be doing, then we're going to have a problem,' Ali Abdaal was telling us. 'It's only a matter of time before you start feeling that sense of meaninglessness and purposelessness.'

Dr Abdaal had experienced the perils of this kind of purposelessness first hand. The first twenty-five years of his life was a list of high-achievers' fantasies: straight As at school, a first-class medical degree from Cambridge and then life on the wards of a London hospital as a junior NHS doctor.

And yet something wasn't right. The truth was, Ali didn't really want to be a doctor at all – it was just the 'high-achieving' default. The more time he spent on the wards, the more he felt a creeping sense of purposelessness.

By the time we met Ali in 2023, all that was past him. He had quit his first career as a doctor to focus full-time on his business as a world-renowned productivity expert, entrepreneur and most recently the author of a bestselling book, *Feel-Good Productivity*. He was on a mission to help prevent others from falling into the same trap.

We asked how we can learn to recognise this misalignment earlier than he did. His answer was a little macabre. 'One activity I did, was to write out my own obituary. You have to think to yourself: *What would I want my obituary to say?*'

This wasn't as morbid as it sounded, he argued. 'It's so easy for us to get caught up in the day-to-day,' he told us. 'It's like we're driving and all we can see is what's in the headlights. By doing that, we can often end up in a place where we're like, "Wait a minute – how did I end up here?"

> 'It's so easy for us to get caught up in the day-to-day. It's like we're driving and all we can see is what's in the headlights.' Ali Abdaal

'I've spoken to a lot of people in jobs that they don't like where they've been doing it for a long time and waiting for the bonus. Whenever I hear stories like that, I find it really scary because we only have one life. I would really like to do whatever I can to help nudge my life trajectory to a direction that I actually want it to be, and a big part of figuring this out is beginning with the end in mind. What would I want people to say when I'm dying? How can I reverse-engineer that to where I see my life going in the next five years?'

Ali's approach has a strong grounding in science. In fact, a whole body of research has shown again and again that when people are made aware of their mortality they do a better job of prioritising what matters the most to them here and now. In one study, two groups of volunteers were asked to reflect on their deaths before being asked to think about a different topic. In one group, it was taking time to imagine a disaster taking place in their local community; the second group was asked to reflect on the effects of climate change.[1] In both cases, when people were made aware of their own mortality they sought to emphasise being part of something bigger and more durable than themselves – such as their religion or pride in their country.[2] Thinking about death made them more aware of the big things that mattered in life.

Similar studies have found that thinking about our eventual death can inject us with life in any number of different ways – motivating us to exercise more, helping smokers quit and enticing sun worshippers to apply sunscreen more frequently.

Ali Abdaal's 'eulogy method' is doing the same thing. He even offered us his own example. 'Ali Abdaal was one of the world's greatest teachers,' his eulogy began. 'He inspired and educated millions all around the world to build a life they truly love. He holistically combined disciplines from science to philosophy to create an integrated system of living themed around mind, body, heart and soul, which resonated with his loyal following of tens of millions of people all around the world.' When he finished reading the story of his own life, he looked up and smiled. 'This is what I wrote up for my obituary a month ago. I do it every year.'

MICRO-HABITS

Ali Abdaal's method, underpinned by science and personal experience, emphasises the importance of aligning our daily actions with our core values and ultimate goals. His annual exercise of writing his obituary not only helps him stay on course but also serves as a reminder – to him and us – to live a life of significance and joy.

WATCH
THE EPISODE

SIMON SINEK

THE BEST-FRIEND TEST

Simon Sinek is best known as 'the why guy': the world's leading – and bestselling – expert on the power of purpose. When we met him, we wanted to know how he could help us find our own.

He didn't hesitate. 'First of all, understand that your "why" is basically your origin story,' Sinek began. 'It's where you come from. We are all the products of our upbringing – the experiences you had growing up make you who you are. Your "why",' he suggests, 'is fully formed by your mid to late teens and it doesn't change for the rest of your life.'

'Your why is basically your origin story. It's where you come from.' Simon Sinek

The question, then, is how to find our own 'why'. Sinek had an exercise to help. 'Here's a fun way you can learn your "why": it's called a friend's exercise,' he said.

This title is important. 'Go and do this with a best friend,' he cautioned us. 'Do not do this with a spouse. Do not do this with a sibling. Do not do this with a parent. It doesn't work.' The criteria are simple: choose a partner 'who loves you, who will be there for you,' he said. 'They'll pick up the phone at three o'clock in the morning and you would do the same for them.'

The exercise is very straightforward. 'Ask them the simple question: Why are we friends?' He explained what will happen next. 'They're going to look at you like you're nuts, because the part of the brain that controls that deep feeling of love and trust doesn't control language. It's a difficult question to answer, so they'll say, "I don't know." Of course they know. They just don't have the words for it. Ask the question: What specifically is it about me that makes me know that you would be there for me no matter what?'

Sinek urged us to keep pushing through this initial discomfort. 'They'll struggle and you can't help them. You have to let them go through the process, and they'll start describing you: "You're smart, you're loyal, I trust you." You play devil's advocate: "Good. That's the definition of a friend."'

He urged us to continue pressing. 'What, specifically, is it about me that I know you would be there for me no matter what?' Until eventually, you'll get to something more profound.

He described how this verbal dance played out in his own life. 'This is what my friend said to me: "I don't know, Simon. All I do know is that I can sit in a room with you and I don't even have to talk to you. I feel inspired."' His reaction? 'I got goosebumps. In fact, I'm getting them right now,' he said rolling up his sleeve to show us. 'It happens every time. What they did is put the value that I have in the world into words and I had the emotional response.'

This emotional response is what we are all looking for, he argues. 'Somebody will say something and you will either get goosebumps or you'll well up. That's when you know you hit it. Because the thing that you give to the world that you should be working to give to the world consistently is the reason those people love you.'

Sinek is right to argue that deep, meaningful conversations with our friends is the key to working out what matters to us. There is increasingly compelling evidence that strong friendships are dramatically more important than we might think: according to one analysis of thirty-eight studies, adult friendships – especially high-quality ones that provide social support and companionship – are a key guard against mental health problems including depression and anxiety.[1] In contrast, the effects of poor-quality friendships is equivalent to smoking twenty cigarettes a day, according to one analysis of more than 300,000 people.[2]

So make use of these relationships and use them to establish what matters to you. 'If you do this with multiple friends, the amazing thing is they will say very similar things, because that's the thing you give to the world,' Sinek says. 'That is your "why". It's the reason you get out of bed in the morning.'

WATCH
THE EPISODE

3

How to Focus on What Matters

MICRO-HABITS

Life is a game. It's your choice whether you play to win.

WILL GUIDARA

SWEATING THE SMALL STUFF

Will Guidara was staring intently at a hot dog. The sausage we had procured for one of the world's leading restaurateurs was not designed to torment him. It was instead our attempt to entice him into telling us how he created the culture that led to his New York restaurant – Eleven Madison Park – becoming the highest-rated in the world, famous for the creativity of its food and the hospitality of its staff.

Guidara recounted a story of four 'foodies' – fans of high-end establishments – who were dining at his restaurant after a week of sampling the best of New York's food scene. Guidara, who was tidying away the first course, heard one of the party casually mention that during their trip the only thing they hadn't eaten was a genuine New York City hot dog. He saw it as an opportunity and rushed out to buy 'a dirty water dog' from a street vendor, brought it back to the kitchen, dressed it up beautifully and served it as a surprise final course. The group was blown away. 'What was the thing they remembered most?' he asked us. The hot dog, of course.

His point was simple. You can find moments of magic anywhere. And if you look for the small moments of magic, and then capture them, you can instil joy in everybody you meet.

'We all do amazing things randomly,' Guidara said. 'You have to hold on to them, to grab on to them, to put systems behind them. To make sure they keep on happening.' These unexpected moments of magic must be spotted and deliberately replicated, he says. 'Culture is caught, not taught,' is how he puts it.

'We all do amazing things randomly. You have to hold on to them, to grab on to them, to put systems behind them.' Will Guidara

Guidara had an endless list of moments to illustrate the power of seeking out magic. He recounted observing a nine-year-old boy reluctantly nibbling at his food while the rest of his family heartily tucked in to the *haute cuisine*. His eyes shined with delight as he recalled the moment one of his team suggested making a tasting menu specifically for him.

They whipped up a series of playful, unexpected courses: a gourmet grilled cheese, a mini cheeseburger, chicken nuggets. Each one was presented with the same elegance and ceremony as the adult dishes. As the family was leaving, the maître d' handed the boy a menu designed just for him – printed and bound.[1]

Still, if this is a simple course of action it is not always an easy one – as, one suspects, the kitchen hand tasked with making that printed menu might attest. 'It almost breaks my heart,' he says, frowning, 'how many little moments of organic brilliance just kind of flutter away, never to be seen again ... Because people didn't know to hold on to them when they happened the first time.'

For Guidara, the question is how to create systems that ensure that these little instances of creative magic crop up organically. He outlined the three steps he took to ensure these moments could be captured, codified and continuously repeated within his restaurant. They are relevant for anyone who is interested in building something – be it a product, a service or a culture – that people truly love.

The first step is to simply be present, he says. 'Which is an annoyingly overused phrase these days – but in hospitality, it's everything. Being present just means caring so much about the person you're with that you stop caring about everything else you need to do.

'Too often, people are so focused on efficiency that they miss out on the things happening right in front of them. If I was optimising for efficiency when I was clearing their table I would have been scanning the dining room, trying to figure out what other tables I needed to clear, and in what order I needed to clear them. Had I been doing that, I never would have heard that throwaway line about the hot dog.'

The second is to take the task before you seriously. 'Anyone who wants to be great at anything needs to take what they do seriously,' he said. 'But we need to stop taking ourselves so seriously.' It's a crucial distinction. 'Brands that are trying to so carefully curate and put out into the world get in the way of giving those around them the things that will bring them the most joy. A hot dog is way off-brand in a four-star restaurant.' He holds up the hot dog for us to consider. 'But when you look at how I made them feel, who cares?'

Finally, the trick is to acknowledge people as people. 'If hospitality truly is about making people feel seen, the best way to do it is not to treat them like commodities, but unique individuals.' He went back to the hot dog incident. 'I could have given them a bottle of vintage Dom Pérignon, caviar, a Wagyu steak, whatever. It would not have had the same impact as the hot dog because it would not have been specific to them. The greatest connections, the greatest gestures are those where one size fits one.'

This whole project could be distilled down to one simple lesson, relevant to anyone trying to build something and trying to work out where to expend their attention. One of the standard pieces of advice on success in life is to not sweat the small stuff. But when you are trying to create something truly brilliant, the opposite principle holds true: the small stuff makes all the difference.

One of the most influential studies in the science of effective customer service identified five factors that shape our experience: reliability, responsiveness, assurance, empathy and tangibles.[2] The last of these – tangibles – includes things like lighting, uniforms and how a menu feels in the hand. This might sound superficial – it is anything but. They are the tiny cues we use to decide if we're valued, if someone cares, if this is a place worth returning to. In one study, the physical environment of a restaurant – its music, table layout and decor – had a direct impact on how long people stayed, how much they spent and whether they recommended it to others. In another, a hospital's waiting room – just the smell, colour and comfort of the seating – shaped patients' entire perception of the quality of care.

This is why Guidara's hot dog mattered. Not because it was clever. Not because it was funny. But because it said: we saw you, we heard you and we cared enough to act on what you didn't even know you were asking for. That's what the research tells us too.

People don't fall in love with brands, teams or places because of sweeping gestures. They fall in love through the accumulation of small, creative, human moments. Do sweat the small stuff. That's where the magic lives.

WATCH
THE EPISODE

STUART BROAD

ARE YOU PLAYING TO WIN?

Stuart Broad is one of English cricket's greatest-ever fast bowlers. When he retired in 2023, batsmen around the world breathed a little easier knowing that the man who had spent decades tormenting them with his dramatic, game-changing bursts and unshakable levels of confidence had stepped away from the game.

His captain, Ben Stokes, once declared, 'When the big moments come, Broady is always there.' And, as he stepped on to the stage on the *High Performance* tour to detail his many career highlights, his calm manner and steely gaze gave us an insight into what many a hapless opponent standing at the opposite end of the crease had felt. A small shiver ran down our spines.

When we discussed the tail end of his storied career, it was inevitable that we would explore the topic of 'Bazball' ('Brendon hates that term,' cautioned Broad), which was more than just a style of play but a full-throttle revolution – one that has transformed England's Test cricket. Head coach

Brendon 'Baz' McCullum, captain Ben Stokes and Broad himself were central characters in this new approach to the most traditional of games. Ditching caution for aggression, England embraced fearless, attacking cricket, smashing records and defying convention while delivering box-office levels of entertainment, self-belief and relentless positivity.

'Brendon took over at a time when we'd won one in seventeen tests,' Broad explained. 'If you're a coach, it's probably a great time to take over, isn't it? You're not going to do any worse. You can really stamp a different mindset on it.'

At its core, Bazball is exactly that – a mindset – one in which bowlers hunt wickets, batters attack from ball one and draws are almost considered an afterthought. How McCullum introduced it was a little more modest. 'He was in the Lord's changing room,' Broad recounted. 'He's not one for PowerPoint presentations. He doesn't do grand speeches. We were just getting ready for training, and he said, "Boys, can I have a couple of minutes? I want us to play attacking cricket. I'm going to back you as players. You're my team. I want us to always have the mindset that if you can take the attacking option, do it."'

Broad explained his interpretation of this command. 'He lives by the saying, "Run towards the danger. Don't back off it." He will always encourage you to sprint towards pressure moments.

'He is a genuine believer that in cricket, to sell tickets, you're fighting against football, theatres, cinemas and museums,' Broad explained. 'People have spent their money to come and watch you. Entertain them.' This edict seeped into the dressing room and the team's whole approach. Broad echoed his coach: 'Fans don't want to see you block it and try to survive. Go and hit boundaries, hit sixes, try and take wickets at every ball. It is quite a freeing way of looking at the game.'

In the early months of this newly decreed way of playing, it was driven by a combination of McCullum's relentless positivity and his refusal to be swayed by the occasional setback. 'I've never heard him say one negative word; not once,' Broad recalled. 'That's really important because if he comes out and says, "Play without fear. I'm going to back you," then if you get out, he goes "Crap shot. Why did you play that?" then the whole thing's blown.'

Our guest smiled broadly as he shared the occasion when he knew this mindset had taken hold. It was at a critical juncture in the 2022 Nottingham Test match between England and New Zealand. England were trailing their rivals by 280 runs. Captain Ben Stokes enquired of the coach what their approach should be. 'If we lose a wicket, what's my job?' he asked. 'Am I shutting up shop? Am I going for the draw?'

McCullum's reply was unequivocal. 'We're going for the win at all costs. I don't believe in draws,' he told the assembled players. Broad explains that he instructed every player to stand up and look out of the dressing room windows. He made everyone look at Trent Bridge and the full house. 'These guys have spent money to come and watch. They don't want to see you block the ball. Go and win the game.'

This moment helped cement the newly aggressive mindset. 'We won the game,' he explained, 'but it was such a crucial moment because it was the coach saying what he wanted and then a senior player went and delivered it. It just gave the whole group such belief that anything was possible. We went on a run of winning ten out of the next eleven games.'

There is a powerful lesson here. All over the world, in every area of discipline, from academics to sport to music, millions of pounds and thousands of hours are spent on identifying those people who can produce results like McCullum's. But most of these talent-identification programmes are little better than rolling a dice.

Part of the problem with many assessment tools is that they don't actually predict performance. Many of these psychometric tests will inform you about attributes, such as your degree of introversion or extroversion, or the balance you place on thinking versus feeling. These results indicate what you *like* to do. They tell you very little about whether you are actually any good at it, let alone how you can improve if you're not.

According to the psychologists Edward Tory Higgins and Heidi Grant Halvorson, there is a simpler way of establishing whether you are on track for success. They advocate grouping people into two types on the basis of one big personality attribute, which gives a more accurate prediction of performance: are you promotion-focused or prevention-focused?[1]

Those who are promotion-focused concentrate on the rewards that will accrue when they achieve their goals. In short, they play to win. In contrast, those who are prevention-focused see their goals through the lens of responsibilities. They concentrate on staying safe. They worry about what might go wrong if they don't work hard enough or aren't careful enough. They are hyper-vigilant and hang on to what they have. In other words, they play to not lose. No prizes for guessing which mindset McCullum was trying to inculcate in his team.

There is not a hierarchy between the two types of motivation – it is simply that each one is suited to a different type of role. One study of over 200 athletes from a wide range of different sports found that attackers tended to possess promotion focus whereas those tasked with defending tended to be prevention-focused.[2] Psychologists suggest that while many people intuitively choose jobs that suit their outlook best, 'Studies show that prevention-focused individuals are likely to take up what organisational psychologists call "conventional and realistic" work, as administrators, bookkeepers, accountants, technicians and manufacturing workers,' one study concludes. Whereas 'the promotion-focused are likely to pursue "artistic and investigative" careers, as musicians, copywriters, inventors and consultants. These tend to be think-outside-the-box jobs, in which people are rewarded for creative and innovative thinking and being practical isn't emphasised.'[3]

However, it is possible to nudge people from one type of motivation to the other. In fact, it can be accomplished with surprisingly simple tweaks in the language you use to describe a challenge. In one study on this subject, semi-professional soccer coaches in Germany were told to prepare their players to take penalties by using one of two statements: 'You are going to shoot five penalties. Your aspiration is to score at least three times.' Or, 'You are going to shoot five penalties. Your obligation is to not miss more than twice.'[4]

You probably wouldn't expect such a minor tweak to affect a player's performance. In fact, it had a huge impact.

ARE YOU PLAYING TO WIN?

Players did significantly better when the instructions they received were framed according to their dominant motivational focus, which the researchers had previously measured. This was especially true for those players who were more prevention-minded. They scored nearly twice as often when they received the command to 'not miss'.

Whether he realised it or not, this is precisely the toolkit that McCullum was drawing upon. England had for a long time been playing in a prevention-based style, when in fact they were naturally better suited to playing in a promotion-based style. By nudging the players towards a more natural style of play he transformed their results for the better.

It's a lesson we can all learn from. As McCullum might say, life is a game. It's your choice whether you play to win.

WATCH
THE EPISODE

BRIAN COX

FOCUS ON WHAT YOU DON'T KNOW

'A lot of people talk with great confidence about how the universe began,' Britain's favourite physics professor was telling us. 'But how can you? Nobody knows! We don't know yet.'

Professor Brian Cox – physicist, science populariser and former member of nineties pop band D:Ream – was telling us about the power of admitting what you don't know. 'If you can say, "I don't know," that's great for everyone,' he said.

'In certain professions, it's good to know what you're doing.' A pilot, a surgeon, an operator of a nuclear reactor. But the rest of us would do well to adopt the mindset of scientists, who see things very differently. 'If you look at how our reliable knowledge was acquired, it was acquired by people starting from the basis they *didn't* understand. And then the moment that some new data, new evidence, new observation appears that conflicts with your picture of the world, then you start to become interested; you start to be excited. If I'm wrong, then I'm delighted because I've learned something. You have to be delighted when you're shown to be wrong because you've learned something.'

What would it mean to embrace this approach if we aren't scientists, we asked? Cox's answer was instant. 'I think it's pretty simple. It's almost rewarding people for being wrong.' He expanded. 'Part of making things better is recognising when you're wrong.'

'Part of making things better is recognising when you're wrong.' Brian Cox

It's a pity, then, that knowing what you don't know is so often undervalued. Our society places a great premium on confidence and certainty; much less on fallibility and humility. As Cox puts it: 'We have to be less confident in our answers and better at asking.' He suggests that his own work as a scientist was the best training ground for this. 'I spent most of my time actually learning how to be wrong.'

Cox isn't the only one who appreciates the importance of acknowledging how little you know. Social psychologists from Duke University conducted a fascinating study with over 150 participants. To begin, they were all assessed. Some of the people were classed as being intellectually humble: they conceded their opinions weren't always right and were happy to change their stance once presented with new evidence. Others were labelled as intellectually arrogant, claiming they were rarely wrong and never had cause to reconsider their opinions.[1]

They were then issued with three tasks. First they read a series of statements about emotive topics, such as same-sex marriage and the legitimacy of chemical weapons in warfare. The next step was to have them rate their level of knowledge on various subjects. One thing they were unaware of was that one-third of these subjects, like 'Hamrick's Rebellion', were completely made up. They were then asked to remember which of the sixty statements on the second list they had read earlier and which ones were new. On every response, they had to rank their degree of confidence.

The results were clear. The highest scorers on intellectual humility were those who were far more open to hearing opposing opinions and to looking for information that challenged their own thinking. When they got a question wrong, they showed greater self-awareness of it and then paid closer attention to the evidence. Above all, the humble minds were more inclined to admit their errors and own up to their mistakes.

On the other hand, those identified as intellectually arrogant were observed to skim-read through the information, were less accurate at recognising new statements and possessed a greater degree of conviction in the accuracy of their responses; in other words, they didn't know what they didn't know.

Social psychologists have learned that people with higher levels of intellectual humility – i.e. who focus on what they don't know, rather than what they do – tend to be more high performing. In a *Journal of Management* study of over one hundred companies, intellectually humble CEOs were not only easier to work with – sharing their authority, employing more diverse management teams and giving people the opportunity to lead and innovate – they also created tangibly better organisations, with lower staff turnover, increased employee satisfaction and better overall performance.² If these are the benefits of learning to be wrong, who wants to be right?

WATCH
THE EPISODE

BARRY HEARN

WHAT STORY ARE YOU TELLING YOURSELF?

Not many people would associate snooker with storytelling, but it is an art that Barry Hearn has spent his entire career perfecting.

His position as Britain's leading sports promoter – with a background in snooker, and encompassing football, boxing, darts and even fishing – has been spent telling compelling stories that hook an audience: enough that they will pay their hard-earned money to discover what happens next. Sports promotion, at its core, *is* storytelling. It's not just about selling an event but creating characters, building tension, bringing out the stakes – all so people will keep coming back for their next ticket.

His background as a storyteller comes through in spades. When we sat down for his *High Performance* episode, Hearn was filled with anecdotes about what he had learned in four decades as a promoter – tying each one of them to a surprising lesson about his values.

WHAT STORY ARE YOU TELLING YOURSELF?

Consider the time he inadvertently launched the career of one of the best snooker players of his generation. 'No matter how bright you are or how well qualified you are, we all need that bit of luck – and to know how to take advantage of that,' he told us. He offered the example of 'a ginger kid just knocking on my door, saying, "Can I play in one of your snooker tournaments, Mr Hearn?"' He decided to take a chance on him. It paid off. That boy was Steve Davis – and so began one of the most productive working relationships of his career, in which he would see Davis win six world titles. Hearn's not-so-flattering lesson from the incident: 'It's better to be lucky than good looking.'

Another of his rules was even simpler: Tell the truth – it's easier than telling lies. 'It is the most refreshing thing to be able to do,' he told us. 'When you do, those that appreciate it will love you for it. And those that don't, you don't really want to be in their company anyway.' To illustrate his point, he gave us the example of the time he turned down a £30 million offer for his business, Matchroom. When he told his wife about the potential buyers, he described them as 'loud, aggressive Americans. They banged the chair and the desk.'

His wife asked him whether he was sure that he wanted to sell – and it got him thinking. 'The following day, I phoned them up and said "the deal's off,"' he recalled. 'I told them the truth. I said, "I don't like either of you and I don't really want to work with people like you. In fact, I don't even want people like you in my world."' The effect on Hearn was instant. 'I felt like I'd been baptised again. It makes you feel good about yourself. If you don't feel good about yourself, how do you expect other people to feel good about you?'

His final story – and his best one – was told with an undisguised relish, and related to his constant willingness to adapt. 'In 1989, I'm losing millions of pounds and owe the bank millions of pounds,' he said. 'It was my job to fix it. I needed a sponsor and I didn't have one . . . The dreams of what I was thinking my life was gonna be clearly wasn't happening.'

He had one last shot at raising the money he needed. 'I got off at the train station to see my last chance, a managing director,' Hearn said. 'It was Christmas Eve, four o'clock. I got off the train and it started to snow. It was like a Dickens novel.' And like a tragic Dickens character, his pitch fell on deaf ears. 'My heart wasn't in it at all. I started the sales pitch, which I'm generally quite good at, but this was awful. I'd had too much of a battering. I'd lost too many deals.' His audience – a hotel chain chief executive – sensed his desperation. 'He looked at me and said, "It's Christmas Eve, it's 4.30 p.m. You must really need this."'

Hearn applied one of his own rules – tell the truth – and admitted that he was in trouble. His potential client explained that while he couldn't offer him money, he would agree to provide a significant number of hotel rooms, to the equivalent of his sponsorship deal, instead. 'We shook hands and I left,' Hearn recalled. 'By the time I had walked back to the station I'd sold the lot to a mate of mine in the travel business. I got £180,000, which saved my life, saved my business – and saved me.'

This story helped him identify one of his most important rules. He explained, 'It taught me that when you're in situations like that, the situation will define you as a person as well as you will define the situation. *You learn more about yourself in adversity than you'll ever learn in success.*'

We were intrigued by Hearn's remarkable knack for telling compelling stories – and using them to identify life lessons that the rest of us can apply. He never once hectored us with condescending suggestions – he instead took us into his life, and used his own experiences to get us to reflect on our own. And it offered a powerful lesson about how to work out our own priorities in our careers – and in our lives.

This make sense. Stories are uniquely powerful in helping us navigate ambiguous situations. In fact, humans are hard-wired to find stories everywhere. In one famous experiment, the psychologist Fritz Heider[1] and his research assistant Marianne Simmel produced a short animated film, showing a small triangle, a big triangle and a small circle moving busily around a rectangle. They showed the film to over one hundred research participants who were then asked to describe what they saw. Virtually all the observers described the movements by using stories. Many saw a love story, others were convinced that they'd seen a family drama while others viewed it as a slapstick comedy, like *The Three Stooges*.[2] The Heider–Simmel study highlighted humans' strange ability to find narrative in everything.

So it stands to reason that when we hear a story with a clear lesson, like those told by Hearn, we are more likely to understand its implications than if we are simply presented with hard facts. Indeed, the neuroscientist Paul J. Zak has performed extensive research on storytelling and its effects on behaviour and discovered that character-driven stories not only elicit a physiological response, but they also inspire changes in behaviour.

When we listen to information, like a dull presentation containing bullet points outlining our team's abstract values, a part of our brain called the 'Wernicke's area' is activated to translate the words into meaning.³ That is all about what happens with the information. Yet when we hear a story our brains begin to change dramatically. Not only are the language processing parts of it activated, but the brain also releases the exact same chemicals it would if you were actually in the story yourself.

Zak's argument has been bolstered by studies from around the world. Stories are a highly effective way of understanding the world and making sense of our own experiences of it. Stories help break down complexities, exploring big themes like explaining the values that are most important to us. And, as Barry Hearn so skilfully demonstrated, harnessing the power of storytelling provides leaders with the ultimate sweet spot when trying not only to impart information but to work out what really matters to you and your team – and to focus on it above all else.

WATCH
THE EPISODE

How to Organise Your Time (and Your Life)

MICRO-HABITS

If everything is a priority, nothing is.

SHANE PARRISH

SHOW ME YOUR CALENDAR

When we met Shane Parrish he was swaddled in a large winter coat that had survived several bitter Ottawan winters. As he began to unwrap himself, he glanced furtively around the room in anticipation of our interview. He looked like a character from a John le Carré novel.

That was fitting enough, because before becoming a blogger and expert on decision-making Shane Parrish was an intelligence officer. Born and raised in Canada, he was working at a 'three-letter intelligence organisation' – he still can't say which one – during 9/11 and its fallout. In his book, *Clear Thinking*,[1] he describes the mental models and probing questions he had learned to ask of himself when he was on the frontlines of the war on terror – and later when he founded his acclaimed blog *Farnam Street*.

One of his interviewers, Damian, had completed one of *Farnam Street's* online courses, named 'Decisions by Design'.

But when he complimented Parrish on the depth and practicality of the programme, Parrish wasn't interested in praise. 'Thanks,' he responded. 'What could be better about it?'

It was a simple exchange, but beneath the words Parrish was demonstrating a simple but effective method: focusing on his priorities. 'How many priorities do you have?' he asked, letting the question hang in the air for a moment. 'If everything is a priority, then nothing is a priority.'

'If I can't distinguish my top two or three priorities from everything else, one of the symptoms is feeling I have to give my everything to everything. But,' – he paused again – 'you can't give your everything to everything. And when you try, the first thing to go is *you*.'

'You can't give your everything to everything.' Shane Parrish

'What I mean by that, is you start sacrificing your health, your sleep, your mood, your workouts. You start sacrificing the core things that determine whether you are on easy or hard mode. Everything gets harder and harder and it feels like a grind.'

'If you're spreading your time into ten blocks a day, and you spread them over ten projects, that's one block of time a day per project. You're not going to move very fast. You're going to feel busy, but you're not going to get anywhere.'

So what should we do instead? He looked deep into our eyes to land his point. 'You need to narrow things down to two or three priorities. These are your focus and if building a relationship and maintaining that relationship with your partner matters to you, I should be able to see that in your calendar. So don't tell me your priorities. Show me your calendar.'

This powerful insight was learned on the job, he explained. 'When I worked at the intelligence agency, I used to block off an hour or two in the morning just for me,' Parrish said. 'I booked a meeting with myself so nobody could overbook that meeting. That was the most effective hour each day. I did more work in that one hour than I did in the other seven, eight, nine, ten hours at work. It didn't matter. That hour was mine. It was untouchable.'

Parrish's probing questions were more than just intuitively helpful. They also had a strong grounding in science. Indeed, humans' consistent tendency to overfill their calendars – and thereby fail to prioritise what really matters – has been shown scientifically. In one study, titled 'Doing Unto Future Selves as You Would Do Unto Others' psychologists tracked the behaviour of university students who were asked to give up some time to help support and tutor other students who were struggling.[2]

One group was asked to promise to give up time during the current term; another group was requested to do so during the next term. The researchers found a significant difference in generosity between the present and the future commitments. Those asked how much time they would be willing to commit in the present offered just twenty-seven minutes on average, while those asked to commit during the following term responded with an average of eighty-five minutes.

This is a common mistake many of us make. When was

the last time you promised to commit to a new request even with a full calendar looming? We often presume that 'future you' will have far more capacity and drive than 'present you'.

Then, when the time comes to really do the thing we promised, we put our present comfort ahead of our future well-being. When considering jobs to do, we often build narratives about how tough or uninteresting or unpleasant they will be. Still, we also persuade ourselves that tomorrow will be different; *we* will be different tomorrow.

The solution is simple: take a leaf out of Shane Parrish's book and only schedule in the things in a month that you would be just as happy to do today. Who you become is little more than how you choose to spend your time. If you're not prioritising the things that matter, you're choosing to become somebody you don't want to be.

WATCH
THE EPISODE

USAIN BOLT

TRANSFORM YOUR MINDSET

The fastest man of all time was in no hurry.
    Usain Bolt ambled across the stage, seemingly oblivious to the three thousand guests waiting, rapt, to hear his words of wisdom. Known for the outsized personality that lit up Olympic stadiums, he cut a more subdued character in person – only his warm smile and firm handshake giving away his famous charisma. But the greatest contrast came when he opened his mouth. Rather than dwell upon his blaze of world records and his place in sporting immortality, he wanted to emphasise the importance of defeat.

That was because he wasn't always the world champion, Bolt told us. 'I was fifteen when I won the World Juniors,' he began. 'I was really young. I was really talented, so I didn't have to work hard. It was just talent. I was winning and winning and winning.' But before long his early success came to a juddering halt. 'When I got to the professional levels, I felt like it was just going to be easy,' Bolt said. 'I would go to a meet and I would lose and I was like, "This is strange. This is new." It took me a while to understand.'

As a teenager, he travelled with the Jamaica team to the 2004 Olympic Games in Athens – a little-known fact, Bolt said. 'If you didn't follow my career, a lot of people did not know that I went to that Olympics,' he laughed. The reason, perhaps, is the forgettable nature of his performance. 'I thought I was ready, as always, because of my talent. I did well at the Jamaican trials and then got to the Olympics and met up with all these guys that had been training all year round and being dedicated to their craft. I didn't even make it out the first round.' Bolt trailed home fifth.

But if his appearance was forgettable to the public, it was unforgettable to him. 'That was a little bit of a wake-up call to say, "Listen, you have a long way to go." If you can't make it out the first round at the Olympics and there's three more rounds, that shows how far behind I was.'

Indeed, this failure was the making of Bolt. 'No one wants to talk about their failures,' he said. 'But I understand that that's what helped me to get better. If it's one thing I've learned, it's if you can be truthful to yourself, that's how you get better.'

He gave us an example from early in his career to show us what he meant. At the 2007 World Championships in Osaka, Japan, Bolt arrived feeling much more confident in his preparation – and ready to try for gold. But in the end he left with only a silver medal.

'I came second and I went to my coach,' Bolt recalled. 'I said, "I really tried. I really worked."' His coach, the veteran trainer Glen Mills, disagreed 'No, you didn't work hard.

You didn't go to the gym every day. You missed a few days. A couple of days throughout the year and it adds up to a month.' Mills left his disappointed protégé with a simple lesson: 'You have to learn how to lose before you can learn how to win. When you figure this out, you will get better.'

Bolt was perplexed. 'That was one of the biggest things that confused me. I was like, "Why would I want to learn how to lose?"' But eventually, he understood the lesson. 'When you fail, what do you learn from the failure? When you lose, what do you need to do to get better? Over time, I started understanding – this is very important. If you can be truthful to yourself when you lose and say, "All right, I didn't train hard enough, I didn't do the research, I didn't sleep well. Next time I'll do those things and get better and better and better and improve till I get to the top."'

'When you fail, what do you learn from the failure? When you lose, what do you need to do to get better?' Usain Bolt

When he started really interrogating his failure, Bolt started to see the problem. 'Consistency is everything. The problem with me was I would train for two or three weeks, but then I would want to go out and hang out with my friends and take a week off,' he said. 'In my mind that wouldn't affect anything, but it does when you break the pattern and you break the consistency of work.'

Once he realised this he became able to do better. 'You can see the difference in one year,' he said. 'I was very slim, with no muscles. It was all about consistency and strength for me – they go together. In the next year, I really consistently trained and I never missed days. Some days, even when I was sick, my coach would say, "You'll be fine. A little bit of running will help you."'

This consistent discipline eventually took Bolt to the Olympic arena in the 2008 Beijing Games. When he assumed his position in the starting blocks, he was a different athlete. On 16 August 2008, in an incredible race, not only did he win the Olympic 100-metre gold medal, but he left the sporting world scrambling to make sense of what they had just seen: Bolt set a new world record of 9.69 seconds, in just forty-one steps, with an untied shoelace, and managed to start celebrating before he had actually crossed the finish line.

A performance psychologist would have no trouble making sense of Bolt's transformed performance, though – it reflects a classic insight into how we learn from failure.

Whenever we experience a defeat, we experience a stress response: our testosterone levels drop while our cortisol goes up. This tends to increase anxiety, causing us to be more cautious and afraid to take on the next challenge, meaning we tend to perform worse at the next attempt. In contrast, when we win our testosterone spikes, causing us to feel increasingly confident and willing to take more risks; we are actually primed to perform better. This effect has been widely observed in the animal kingdom, where competition for food confers enhanced status on the most powerful members. The animal that wins in battle rises in rank whereas the losing animal suffers the opposite consequence, moving down the hierarchy. In some animals, this effect is so powerful that it influences who wins the next battle. Winners keep on winning. Losers keep losing.[1]

The same effect holds equally true in human cultures. As Usain Bolt's response to his Athens disaster indicates, when we fail we experience a rise in cortisol, making us apprehensive, anxious and more inclined to look for excuses and avoid facing the real problem.[2] As Steve Magness, the author and long-distance running coach, writes, 'After a loss we often delude ourselves to protect ourselves. And the bigger the game, the more importance assigned to it and the deeper intertwined your sense of self and the outcome is, the more likely you are to experience a surge of cortisol and to default to protection, posturing and deflection following a loss.'[3]

But it doesn't have to be this way. It's possible for each of us to turn these short-term setbacks into long-term successes – just like Usain Bolt. The solution lies in a simple insight developed by the Stanford professor of psychology, Dr Carol Dweck. Dweck once took 330 students aged eleven to twelve and gave them a questionnaire designed to explore their beliefs about talent – and, in particular, their intelligence. From there, she identified who had a 'fixed mindset' – that is, like Bolt's belief that his talent would always be enough, you think the way things are is more or less the way things always will be – as well as those who had a 'growth' mindset, meaning they had faith in their ability to change their behaviour.

Next, the students were presented with a sequence of challenges. The first eight were relatively straightforward, but the following four became significantly more demanding.

As the children pressed on, a striking pattern began to appear. Those in the fixed-mindset group hit a wall when faced with the more complex puzzles. Rather than rising to the challenge, they began to question their own capabilities, attributing their struggles to a lack of natural ability. Comments like 'Maybe I'm just not that clever,' 'I've never had a good memory,' or 'This kind of thing just isn't for me,' began to circulate. Their faith in their own ability crumbled as the tasks grew tougher.

The growth-mindset group, however, reacted quite differently. They didn't internalise the setbacks as personal failings. In fact, they didn't even frame their struggle as failure – they saw it as an opportunity to stretch themselves. They embraced the tougher puzzles with curiosity and enthusiasm. And, crucially, this mindset helped them outperform their fixed-minded peers by the end of the task.

The contrast was not just dramatic, it was extraordinary. The difference in performance had nothing to do with genetics, intelligence or motivation. It came down to one simple thing: the difference between two mindsets.

Here's the key takeaway: when you believe you *can* find a solution, your chances of doing so increase dramatically – just like Usain Bolt, who only began to fulfil his true potential when he accepted that raw talent wasn't enough and he had to commit to focused, sustained training. As Carol Dweck puts it: 'In the growth mindset, you don't feel the need to convince yourself and others that you have a royal flush when you are secretly worried it's a pair of tens. The hand you're dealt is just the starting point.' [4]

TRANSFORM YOUR MINDSET

This realisation has powerful implications for how we respond to failure. If we want to overcome challenges, we must first expand our belief in what we're capable of. Just like Usain Bolt, only when we embrace failure – and even learn from it – can we hope to thrive. By learning to lose, we learn to win.

WATCH
THE EPISODE

TOM DALEY

PROCESS GOALS BEAT OUTCOME GOALS

Tom Daley is the Peter Pan of British diving, still youthfully exuberant after fifteen years at the top of his sport. He started his career at the tender age of thirteen and has been part of five Olympic cycles, which have garnered one gold, a silver and three bronze medals. How does he do it?

It began in 2004, he told us. He described how, at the age of ten, he had started drawing the medals he was winning in local diving competitions in a sketchbook, at the encouragement of his father. 'In the front of it, I drew a picture of myself in a handstand in front of LONDON 2012. That was when London was only a candidate city and it hadn't even been announced that it was the host.' Daley says that this drawing was his first attempt at 'visualising where I wanted to be and visualising how I could get there. I just knew what I wanted and would not stop at anything to make it happen.'

Visualisation is a powerful tool, and Daley would spend

PROCESS GOALS BEAT OUTCOME GOALS

the next few years fine-tuning his visualisation method. 'The main difference is now, I don't write outcome goals,' Daley told us – things like 'compete at London 2012'. These, he has discovered, 'are a slippery slope', because they are not within our gift. 'If I was to write down "win the world championships", that is too much focused on the outcome and an outcome you can't control,' Daley said.

Instead, he focuses on process goals: specific things he wants to do that will help him move towards the desired outcome – but which he is in absolute control of. 'The only thing you can control is the process,' he says, 'so controlling the controllable and focusing on what you need to do to get to where you want to be.'

That is why, to this day, every morning Daley focuses on three small things he can control – and uses them as the basis for his routine. 'Every morning I'll write three things down that I want to do. Sometimes it's just reminders, but sometimes it's a goal that I want to do for the day. For example, I'm going to be doing my twisting dive on a three-metre board. I want to stay positive when I go into the pool. I know I've got a hard gym session before it, and sometimes after a hard gym session you can feel like you're not going to have the best pool session.' His list also contains pragmatic goals. 'I also make sure that I pick up some milk on the way home.' The important thing is the manageable number of targets. 'There'll always be three things I write down every day that I want to achieve.'

Daley told us that this focus on easily controllable process goals has been integral to his success. He described a difficult moment during London 2012. 'There was a lot of expectation and a lot of pressure,' he told us. 'I felt it a lot. I remember standing there thinking, *There are 18,000 people watching here and millions watching at home. There's a billboard on the Mall with my face on it and I'm about to do six dives that I've trained for for four years. I get one shot at this.*' This fractured focus affected his performance, and in the preliminary rounds he finished a disappointing fifteenth.

But then, in the final, he reminded himself of his simple maxim: set goals that you can control, and cut out everything else. 'I got to the semi-final and [asked myself], "Why am I doing this, if I'm not enjoying it?",' he said. 'To compete in an Olympic Games in front of a home crowd is something that so few people will ever get to experience.' He defined one of his three targets as: 'I'm just going to have fun; enjoy it and just let it rip. Going into the final, instead of being worried about what might go wrong, I was just going to go out there and enjoy it and dive and have fun.'

He described the effect of this focus as he stepped up to take his final dive. 'I knew I was in medal contention and as I walked to the end of the diving board, the cheers were deafening. The whistle blew and it went completely silent. There was nothing. Because it was so loud before, all you could hear was the water going down the drains. I looked down and saw the Olympic rings on the bottom of the pool: London 2012. I just remember this switch in my head . . . I found a sense of flow and I just knew what I was doing and I didn't have to overthink it.' Focusing on goals he could control had saved his career.

PROCESS GOALS BEAT OUTCOME GOALS

Tom Daley is not the only one to have realised the perils of outcome-oriented goals. Many weight-loss studies have found that when participants who are dieting to solely lose a certain amount of weight occasionally slip up and eat badly they were more likely to abandon their whole diet. In contrast, those dieters who were focused on the small steps and on enjoying the process of eating more healthily were more likely to continue with their healthy habits. As a result, the people who focused *less* on achieving their outcome were more likely to meet it.[1]

Other research on financial saving plans and students revising for exams found similar results. Participants who missed a financial goal they were saving for were more likely to then splurge and overspend than those who hadn't, and when students who were fixated on achieving a certain grade missed a deadline for an assignment they were more likely to fail the whole subject rather than complete it at all.[2]

On the other hand, those who – like Daley – focus on process tend to achieve more success. In their 2011 book *The Progress Principle*, Professor Teresa Amabile and Steven Kramer describe getting 238 workers from twenty-six project teams across seven businesses to keep an anonymous diary so that they could document their everyday experiences. They collected almost 12,000 journal entries, which they used to examine people's 'inner work lives' – their perceptions, feelings and motivation levels – and how this affected their performance.

They discovered that when people take continuous, small steps forwards on important tasks they become more creative, productive and engaged, as well as having better relationships. In other words, the Peter Pan of diving was right: focusing on the 'small wins' is the key not only to success but a happy life at work and beyond.

WATCH
THE EPISODE

SABRINA COHEN-HATTON

THREE QUESTIONS FOR BETTER DECISIONS

Each one of us makes between 30,000 and 35,000 decisions every day. But we aren't always very good at making them, particularly when the pressure is on. In one recent study, scientists found that when we're in high-stakes situations we are 'more likely to be aware of things that have been rewarding and to overlook information predicting negative outcomes'.[1] In other words, under pressure we become guided by illogical prejudices that support the information we want rather than the information we need – and our decision-making suffers as a result.

This is something that Dr Sabrina Cohen-Hatton knows better than most. A senior firefighter, she has spent her career surrounded by people making decisions – sometimes good, sometimes bad – that often had life-or-death consequences. One day, a few years into her time in the fire service, she was called to a fire that had potentially injured her husband – and it made her appreciate just how rattled our decision-making faculties become when the stakes are high.

The experience got her thinking: Why are we so often so bad at making the most important decisions? And how can we improve? Such questions prompted Sabrina to undertake a PhD in behavioural neuroscience, alongside her main job of battling infernos. And it soon started to pay dividends.

She came to realise that there was something unique about decisions that are made under intense pressure. 'I think most people who work in high-pressured environments will tell you that at the time that you're going through something you don't have the time and the space for self-doubt,' she said. 'You focus on the task at hand, you do what you need to do. And it's usually afterwards, when it's quieter, when the self-doubt can creep in.'

These self-doubts, she argues, can be paralysing. 'When you are making those big decisions you can experience something called decision inertia. This happens in situations that can be really uncertain or where you are overly focused on anxieties about your own accountability.' She offered us a simple analogy to illustrate the difference. 'It's like throwing a pebble in a pond. If you're constantly thinking about the ripples, you lose sight of the pebble and where it's landed.'

So, what does a focus on how we make decisions under pressure tell us about making better choices in the rest of our lives, we asked? Her answer homed in on a simple, science-based method called 'decision controls' – a set of simple questions designed to make better high-stakes judgements, and rooted in her experience as a firefighter.

THREE QUESTIONS FOR BETTER DECISIONS

Number one: What's my goal? 'That might sound really simple,' she said. 'But if you're making a gut decision, you might be making a decision based on a piece of the jigsaw, just a single piece of the situation, which might be the right thing for that, but it could have unintended consequences when you stop and put that piece of the jigsaw back in the bigger picture. Is this going to help me get any further to it?'

Number two: What do I expect to happen? 'That also sounds really simple, but when you are making a gut decision under pressure we found from our research that people's situational awareness is actually quite low,' she argued. 'You're very much focused on the here and now, not on what might happen next or where you're going to be in the next thirty minutes.' This question, she explains, 'is a really effective way of increasing your situational awareness.'

Number three: How does the benefit outweigh the risk? 'Just rationalising that to yourself can help to kick you out of that loop of ... anxieties, and really helps you stand by the decision that you make.'

By asking yourselves these three questions while making hard decisions, you can ensure you're not falling victim to your panicky brain. In fact, Cohen-Hatton maintains these decisions can be successfully employed into any working environment – not only when fighting fires. 'You can do it when you go into the fridge and you're trying to decide whether or not you're going to grab that extra piece of chocolate cake,' she said, running through her decision controls. 'What's my goal? It's to eat healthily. What do I expect to happen? If I eat this cake, it's going to be amazing in the moment, but then I'm going to feel like crap for the rest of the evening, I'm going to feel really guilty and I'm going to have to go for a three-mile run tomorrow, which I really can't be arsed with.

'Is the benefit worth the risk? On reflection,' she laughs, 'probably not. At that point, I reach for a banana.'

WATCH
THE EPISODE

5

How to Connect with Others

MICRO-HABITS

How often do you know what you're *really* talking about?

CHARLES DUHIGG

HUG, HEAR OR HELP?

Charles Duhigg knows how to communicate. A Pulitzer Prize-winning author, he has spent his professional life telling stories – with a particular knack for making complex psychological and behavioural concepts accessible to a broad audience.

So it was fitting that when he sat down in the *High Performance* studio, Duhigg had just penned one of the best books ever written about the art and science of communication. Its name: *Supercommunicators*.

Duhigg's argument was rooted in a simple observation. Each of us knows someone – be it a relative, a friend or a colleague – who just intuitively gets how to communicate well. They know exactly what to say in any situation to both make people feel at ease and elicit a response that will move the conversation forwards. These are the 'supercommunicators'.

Duhigg had a hunch that all of us could learn some tricks from the supercommunicators – not least because we understand them now better than ever. 'We're living through this golden age of understanding communication for really the first time, because of advances in neural imaging and data collection,' Duhigg said. He pointed us in the direction of one study showing that during a powerful conversation, the brains of the speaker and the listener begin to synchronise. Researchers found that this phenomenon – known as neural coupling – happened when a storyteller would vividly describe a personal experience and the listener's brain activity began to mirror the speaker's, particularly in regions related to language, meaning and emotion. When this effect was stronger, the better the listener understood and remembered the story.[1]

So, what is the trick to supercommunication, we wondered? His answer was simple. 'Oftentimes we think a discussion is about one thing,' he said. 'We're talking about sport, or we're talking about our kids. But actually every discussion is made up of different kinds of conversations. And those kinds of conversations tend to fall into one of three buckets.' It raises a troubling question: when you're in conversation, how often do you know what you're *really* talking about?

Duhigg's buckets can help. The first is practical conversations. 'This is where we're making plans and we're solving problems together.'

The second is emotional conversations: 'Where I might tell you how I feel about something and I don't want you to solve my feelings; I want you to empathise.'

Finally, there's social conversations: 'This is about how we relate to each other in society, and the social identities that are important to us.'

He explained why understanding this distinction matters. 'If we're not having the same kind of conversation at the same moment, it's very hard for us to connect. It's very hard for us to hear each other.'

'If we're not having the same kind of conversation at the same moment, it's very hard for us to connect.' Charles Duhigg

He has a simple solution to these kinds of miscommunication, though. And it lies in a simple question: 'Do you want to be hugged, helped or heard?' It is another way of asking: 'Do you want a practical conversation, an emotional conversation or a social conversation?'

Duhigg provided us with a helpful example of how this insight can improve our ability to communicate. 'I fell into this bad pattern with my wife, where I would come home from work after a long day and I'd complain about my work, and my wife would make this very practical suggestion, like, "Why don't you take your boss to lunch, and get to know him a little bit better?"

'Instead of being able to hear what she was saying, I would get even more upset. I would say, "You're supposed to be on my side, you're supposed to be outraged on my behalf!" She would get upset because I was attacking her for giving me good advice.'

But soon they took a leaf from the supercommunicators' book. 'So now what we do is we just ask. When I start complaining about my day, my wife will say, "Do you want me to help you solve this problem or do you just need to vent?"'

MICRO-HABITS

It has had an immediate impact on his relationship. 'It feels really good for someone to ask you what you want, because oftentimes, up until that moment, I haven't thought about it myself.'

It's a tool we can all draw upon. It pays to start your conversations by understanding what your role is: hug, hear or help?

WATCH
THE EPISODE

AJ TRACEY

THE POWER OF YOUR INNER CIRCLE

AJ Tracey isn't just a rapper. He's a one-man movement. Since bursting on to the UK music scene, his razor-sharp way with words and his ability to move seamlessly between musical genres – from grime to garage to Afroswing through to drill – has made him unique. And he has done this as a rare independent artist. He has consistently refused to sign to a major label, staunchly resisted the idea of being mainstream and, instead, held true to a creative freedom and autonomy that many of his peers look upon with envy.

So how did he do it? Well, when we met him he was keen to share one of the most important lessons in doing this: the role of his inner circle. 'First off,' he began, 'you don't pick your friends initially. But there comes a time when your friend group can get stagnant. If you understand that people around you don't have the same ambition as you, it's counterproductive to be around them.'

There was nothing cruel about this approach, he emphasised. 'I don't want to sound like some horrible guy who just cuts off all his friends. I have got the same group of friends that I've had for ten years. It's about knowing how and when to share your energy and time.'

He offered us an intriguing example of how he first came to adopt this approach. 'I had a little music group when I was coming up,' he said. 'When I did my first BBC freestyle, we smashed it. We came out and everyone was on a high. But I took that opportunity to actually scold everyone. That sounds crazy but I'll explain why.

'I said to everyone, "The harsh reality of this is, I know where I'm going. I know what I'm going to achieve. I promise you . . . You have to put in your shift. You have to do it. I'm letting you know, if you want to be with me, come with me."' He wanted more than just that BBC session, he said. 'That was great what we [just] did, but you need to understand that I don't stop here. You achieve something and you've got to keep your foot on the gas.'

This approach has stayed with Tracey throughout his career. He is always on the hunt for evermore impressive people. 'I genuinely believe you should be hanging out with people who, you believe, are achieving more than you,' he said. 'If you're hanging out with people who are achieving less than you . . . That's a problem. You shouldn't be around these people. These people are going to make you feel like it's OK to underachieve. But it's never OK to underachieve.'

AJ Tracey was not the first person to come to this conclusion. The Framingham Heart Study has examined the power of social networks by tracking three generations of residents in Framingham, a city in Massachusetts, since the late 1940s.[1] And it has demonstrated precisely the effect that Tracey identified – we become like the people we spend time with. The research indicated a person was far more likely to become obese if someone in their circle had also become similarly obese – the level of weight gain depended upon the strength of the relationship. If it was a friend the increase in likelihood was 57 per cent, dropping to 40 per cent if it was a sibling and 37 per cent if it was their spouse. Interestingly, the effect was linked to how strongly the individual felt about the other person – if it was someone they didn't have a close relationship with, there was no such correlation. Similar results were found relating to the level of divorce, smoking and drinking alcohol.

The same effects can be seen when it comes to people's performance. In one study, it was discovered that when your friends work hard you will also tend to increase your own personal efforts. Researchers set a series of experiments in which participants performed cognitive tasks while observing others completing similar tasks. The researchers found that mental effort is socially determined. When a student worked on a task in the vicinity of someone else who was also working hard on theirs, the effect was contagious.[2] The same, it seems, is true for intelligence: evidence indicates that your childhood best friends can heavily influence your future IQ scores.

MICRO-HABITS

The famous motivational speaker Jim Rohn once declared that: 'You are the average of the five people you spend the most time with.' AJ Tracey would agree. Friends aren't just there to entertain us – they shape who we are and who we can become. Choose them wisely.

WATCH
THE EPISODE

GEORGE RUSSELL

ASK FOR HELP

'When I was eleven years old I believed I could achieve anything,' George Russell laughed. 'I felt like I could fly to the moon and back, easily.'

It was an entirely understandable position. 'I used to have races where I felt so superior to everyone,' the Mercedes F1 driver told us. He recounted a race during his teenage years where he pinpointed exactly the place – which bend and on which specific lap – he would overtake opponents. 'It was the most stupid thing ever, but I managed to achieve it. I just felt like I could do anything.'

But this arrogance would eventually prove Russell's undoing. 'When I left school at fourteen, I had a similar view. I felt like I could be Formula One world champion before you know it,' he said. 'It was only when I was sixteen that I started to recognise that life isn't as straightforward as that.'

In his later teenage years – when Russell was capturing the British Formula 4 title at his first attempt – his naivety quickly began to catch up with him. He was slow to realise that talent alone was not enough. 'The stars need to align, especially in a sport like ours where there's only twenty race seats available. There's only one or two race seats available every year.' He began to work out his odds. 'I was growing up racing against thousands of different kids, all striving for that same goal. Yet every year there's only going to be one – or two, if you're lucky – who make it to Formula One.'

This realisation forced him to reappraise his strategy. He couldn't simply race fast – he also needed to race smart. 'I thought, *What do I need to do to get an opportunity with an F1 team?*' The answer: ask for help. And ask the help of one person in particular: Toto Wolff.

'I got Toto's address and emailed him,' he explained. 'Toto Wolff is not going to look at British Formula 4 and say, "George Russell, who's won the championship by a couple of points: we need to sign him!"' That meant he needed to be proactive. 'If I put myself in front of him, talk to him and show him what I'm made of, maybe there's an opportunity,' Russell thought.

'I've got nothing to lose. You know, in the worst case, he doesn't reply, in which case I've lost nothing. In the best case, he replies.' His initial request was simply for time. 'I didn't want to go in too hard. I just said, "I'm George Russell. It would be great to meet you and talk about the future."'

Reply he did. 'I sent the email about nine o'clock in the evening,' Russell recounted. 'He replied within fifteen minutes.' Within four weeks, Russell found himself sitting opposite one of the most influential figures in F1.

What did Russell request in this meeting, we asked? 'I

let him feel that he was part of my career,' Russell told us. 'Rather than just disappearing for a year and reappearing, which I think some people would do, he gave me some advice to join a certain team in Formula 3 and said, "We'll keep an eye on you and we'll stay in touch and we'll go from there."'

Russell didn't follow this piece of advice, instead opting to join the British team, Carlin. He wrote to his newly appointed mentor to explain his decision. 'I sent Toto an email saying, "Thanks for your advice . . . I appreciate your opinion. I feel that joining the British team would be better for my future progress."' Wolff was customarily quick to respond: 'I think you're making the wrong decision but best of luck. Let's stay in touch and let's see how you get on.'

Wolff's doubts proved unfounded. Russell's success in his new car gave him the opportunity to continue the relationship. 'I felt like I had a good relationship with him, and I had the confidence a year later to go to him and just have a chat. This was where we picked up the conversation again and that's when I signed a four-year deal for Mercedes.'

Russell's story underlines a mistake we often make when it comes to asking for support. There is a growing body of evidence showing that we tend to grossly underestimate the likelihood that people will assist us, instead focusing on how difficult or unpleasant the request we are making is, worrying about how busy the other person is and fretting about how inconvenient it will be for them to assist.[1] Dale Miller, a psychologist at Stanford University, has consistently demonstrated that when we think about other people's motivation, we tend to apply a more pessimistic, self-interested view about human nature than we would to ourselves.[2]

In fact, people tend to be much keener to give us help and advice than we tend to assume. Dozens of studies have found that people are generally pro-social and keen to make a positive difference, often feeling happier after doing so[3] and even having a more positive view about the competence of the person seeking help.[4] In one study conducted by psychologists, participants were asked to complete a set of puzzles and brain-teasers. Afterwards, some were randomly assigned to ask a colleague for advice on how to improve their performance. The fascinating finding? Those who sought advice weren't judged as being less capable – as many of us might fear – but perceived as more intelligent, thoughtful and respectful.

Why? Their willingness to seek advice was interpreted as a signal of confidence, humility and trust in others' expertise. It is an insight that George Russell would recognise. Seeking help is not a sign of weakness. It is a strategic move – one that can open opportunities that would otherwise remain firmly closed.

WATCH
THE EPISODE

DAN CARTER

HOW TO READ EMOTIONS

What explains the success of the All Blacks, New Zealand's famed rugby team? Some put it down to talent – an endless conveyor belt of world-class players. Others to tradition – the iconic black jersey, the haka, the weight of legacy. Others still to their relentless training and work ethic, where standards are sky-high and no level of detail is too small to perfect. But Dan Carter puts it down to something else entirely: emotional literacy.

Regarded by many as the definitive fly-half of the modern era, Dan Carter was explaining to us how he viewed his role within the set-up. 'We're trying to create a culture and environment that you can be really proud of,' he said. 'Here in New Zealand, we are lucky enough to have this amazing history behind us with rugby union – it's been played here for over one hundred years.'

But it hasn't always been easy. By 2007, the All Blacks had

acquired something of an unwelcome reputation as 'chokers' on the sport's highest stages. In that year's World Cup, they faced France in Cardiff in a legendary quarter-final and were on the wrong end of a 20–18 defeat that would shape the next decade. 'That day, a lot of the team froze,' Carter explained to us. 'The communication was poor, and we started playing within ourselves. Other members of the team went into a state of flight, just wanting to get off the field. A couple of the others went into a state of fight, actually looking for a scrap on the field.'

The defeat prompted a lot of navel-gazing. The coaching staff, Carter and his teammates began asking some searching questions. 'In the first seven years of my career, we spent so much time in the gym, out on the training field, and that's what we thought high performance was – just training harder than anyone else. Little did we realise that we weren't spending enough time on our mental strength.'

His definition of the term? 'High-performance is being able to deal with and have the tools to be able to perform under pressure. We went away and we actually really dived into the reasons why we were unsuccessful. And a lot of it was around pressure. We didn't like pressure.'

This led them to accept that knowledge on this topic was likely to be sourced outside their world. After a rigorous search, they began working with Dr Ceri Evans, a world-renowned former Rhodes Scholar and psychiatrist.[1] The players and coaches formed the 'Mental Analysis and Development Group' – they called it MAD for short – to confront the issue of pressure: what it is, what it does and what they can do about it. 'Once we changed our mindset, all of a sudden we were able to perform,' Carter told us. It was a typical bit of understatement: in the years that followed, the All Blacks became the most successful side in history.

> 'Once we changed our mindset, all of a sudden we were able to perform.' Dan Carter

We asked Carter to share some of the key lessons from his mental gym. He was happy to oblige. His first lesson was to get comfortable with having these vulnerable discussions. 'When I first started playing for the All Blacks,' he recounted, 'if you went and saw a psychiatrist your teammates would look at you and think, "Are you OK, mate? Is everything all right?" It's something you wouldn't do. Now, fast-forward to today's era, if you're not seeing the "head coach" you're teammates are asking "Why not? Do you not want the best out of you?"'

This willingness to explore the inner game then allowed Carter and his teammates to develop a common language: red and blue thinking. It became as much a part of their lexicon as discussing tackling techniques, drop kicks and scrummaging. 'When you're under pressure, you can go into a state of red head where you lose control,' he told us. 'You're not clear and you're not calm. Or you can go into the blue head. In blue, you're calm and clear in your decision-making. In the game, I needed to be in a state of blue as much as possible.'

Carter conceded that learning to spot the switch in colours was integral. 'You can never go through a game of rugby and not go into a red-head state. The key is recognising when you are in red and having the ability to get back into blue as fast as possible.'

How did they learn to get back into the clear-headed place of blue thinking? Carter explained how it helped him react constructively to mistakes. Early in his career, he would often feel anxious after an error. 'I would run around for the next five or ten minutes afterwards thinking, *Don't make that same mistake [again]* or I'd be thinking, *Why did you make that poor pass?*'

Learning to breathe deeply was a simple method of stopping these intrusive thoughts and allowed him to focus on the current, immediate moment. He would combine this with a physical gesture to ground him back into the moment. 'It's a signal to my brain. I would go external to get myself back on track, to get back into a state of blue. If you saw me make a mistake, you'd often see me whack my leg. I'd whack my leg and then go to the next task.' *I need to be present and focus on the next task*, was the inner dialogue he would have.

This new-found emotional literacy on the part of the team was, according to Carter, integral to its success. Suddenly, everyone in the team had a simple framework for making sense of their emotions – and keeping calm under pressure. 'When I was kicking a goal in front of 80,000 people, the last thing I want to be thinking is, *Oh my God, 80,000 people are watching me. What if I miss? I can't miss!*' he said. 'Instead of whacking myself, I'd start pushing my toes into the ends of my boots in the ground for a couple of seconds. I would feel the grass in my toes and then tell myself, "OK. Breathe."

HOW TO READ EMOTIONS

All of a sudden, for five seconds, I haven't thought about missing the kick or all the people that are watching me. I go back to my routine, breathe, visualise the ball going through. It would really help me get back on track and remind myself to live in the now.'

WATCH
THE EPISODE

6

How to Get the Best Out of People

MICRO-HABITS

Without trust, we are nothing.

MARCUS WAREING

SURROUND YOURSELF WITH THE BEST

Marcus Wareing's passion for cooking has its origins in watching his father at work as a fruit and potato merchant in Southport. It was his father who encouraged him to leave the family business and head to London to make his mark within the culinary world. And it was his father's continued advice that showed him how to pull it off.

His wisdom was profane but profound, emphasising the benefits of working hard, being disciplined and, above all, surrounding yourself with the right people. 'Surround yourself with shite, you'll become shite,' was one of his classic pieces of advice, Wareing told us.

How did he learn to do this, we asked? 'I'd pinpoint a couple of people that I wanted to get to their level. I would identify them as soon as I walked into the kitchen.' Then, he would observe them intently. 'Look at them, watch them, make sure they're doing what you like, see what they're all about – and add it to your arsenal of information.'

On occasion, Wareing would employ a bold method to gain membership into these elite environments. Albert Roux, the head chef of Le Gavroche, was a man he wanted to observe at close quarters. The problem was how to reach him. Getting 'from a five-star hotel', where Wareing was employed, 'to a three-star Michelin', where he wanted to be, was no mean feat. 'Like flying from the North Pole to the South Pole,' he said. 'Completely different places.'

So Wareing turned to his father for some advice. 'He asked me, "What are you doing tomorrow?" I said, "I'm off." He said, "I want you to do me a favour. Get up, have a shower, have a shave, put your best suit on and go knock on their door."' Wareing was reluctant. 'I can't go and knock on the Gavroche door,' he said. His father was adamant. 'Will you just fucking do it? Do it for me and see what happens next.' Miraculously, it worked. 'Two weeks later, I got a letter offering me a job.'

When he arrived, he adopted the same mindset which had been inculcated in him back in Southport. 'There was one person in that room, in that kitchen, that just stood out from the crowd, who was completely different from anyone else . . . A cooking machine of pure focus and adrenaline,' Wareing recalled. When he told his dad about him, he responded with his usual wisdom: 'People like that – watch them, focus on them and go with them.' The chef was Gordon Ramsay. 'He was a game changer in that kitchen and he became a game changer in my career, because that was the chef who stood out from any other chef I'd ever worked with.'

SURROUND YOURSELF WITH THE BEST

Wareing Senior's approach to high performance is one that many of the world's leading experts would recognise. 'A great deal of human learning is imitation,' writes Angela Duckworth, a renowned psychology professor and author of the seminal book on the psychology of perseverance, *Grit*. 'We were all born to copy-paste.'[1] She describes a study in which people are encouraged to solve a puzzle – not by working it out by themselves, but by imitating a specific goal-achieving method applied by a friend or colleague. Some participants were given a particular task along with the instruction to copy as much as they liked; others were given no such instruction. It found that simply copying people who had already mastered a task dramatically improved the speed of people's learning.[2]

The same applies in the world of elite kitchens. From Le Gavroche he went on to cook at Pétrus and the acclaimed Marcus at the Berkeley. At every turn, his career illustrates how learning from the best can propel one to exceptional heights in any field.

WATCH
THE EPISODE

SIR IAN MCGEECHAN

ALWAYS SHOUT YOUR ROUND

Sir Ian McGeechan is the Lion King: the player turned coach turned administrator who has taken four disparate teams of the home nations and moulded them into winning units, and doing so under the greatest of pressure.

As we saw in our introduction, his advice is simple. It's about the 'world-class basics': doing the simple, everyday habits as well as you possibly can. And one particular world-class basic has always jumped out to us: shouting your round.

The term is McGeechan's shorthand for taking the steps needed to bring a team together. It was a method he developed while working at the elite level of the sport, coaching the British & Irish Lions. 'It was quarter to one in the morning,' he recounted, describing one early meeting in 2009. 'We'd got everybody in the bar, having a drink, just getting to know each other. They'd only been together two days. I just said, "Let's have a drink and learn a bit more about each other."'

To this day, he says that decision to shout a round of drinks for his team was integral to their eventual success. Without some level of intimacy in a team, it is doomed to failure on the pitch. 'Sometimes it comes down to knowing what you want to do and how you want to do it and the impact it will have on somebody else,' he told us. 'If you keep getting that right, the confidence that other people get from your presence actually just grows.'

This emphasis on building a sense of camaraderie from the ground up was first developed when McGeechan was a young schoolboy, playing rugby alongside much older, more experienced and more hardened men in Leeds. 'It came from my own experience of the support I got,' he said. His father understood the importance of standing your ground on the field and then standing your round at the bar. 'I had a father who put five pounds in my pocket when I was still at school as an eighteen-year-old so that I could buy the rounds and stand at the bar after the game and still be around with everybody else,' he said.

'It comes down to knowing what you want to do and how you want to do it and the impact it will have on somebody else.' Ian McGeechan

McGeechan admitted that it wasn't until his after his father's death that he truly appreciated what his dad had done for him in these moments. 'I didn't know, until after he died, that he had to walk to work for the last two days of the week to afford this money.' But he never forgot the lesson. When asked about the recipe for team success on the podcast, his answer was simple: 'It comes back to the five pounds in the pocket. I'm not going to make a shortcut.'

McGeechan is correct to home in on the importance of strong social connections for the performance of his team. For years, psychologists have been aware of the effects of 'social loafing' – the idea that while all team members are working together to achieve a common objective, each member contributes somewhat less than they would if they were individually accountable – as being corrosive to high-performing teams. Max Ringelmann, a French agricultural engineer, conducted one of the first experiments on social loafing in 1913. Ringelmann was interested in learning how farm workers could increase their production. He created a simple task in which participants pulled on a rope, both individually and then in groups. He discovered that when working in a group, people made less effort than working alone.[1] Why? Because they felt like their contribution wasn't being noticed, and so they could get away with doing less.

But there's a classic way to overcome the power of social loafing. One variation of the original Ringelmann study found that when participants believe their individual contributions are being observed, they work harder – decreasing the loafing effects.[2] When researchers asked two groups of people to brainstorm as many ideas as they could on a given subject, the scientists found that those who felt their contribution was being noticed – and acknowledged – consistently worked harder than those who didn't.

This is precisely what McGeechan was doing, implicitly, when he bought that round for his teammates. It meant that

ALWAYS SHOUT YOUR ROUND

everyone was being recognised for their contribution to the team – and so became keener to do their bit to make it a success. In other words, shouting your round doesn't just make everyone present happier, it makes them more effective teammates, too.

WATCH
THE EPISODE

KEVIN SINFIELD

THE HELPING HAND

Kevin Sinfield is a man who has spent his life raising the bar and then helping others climb over it.

The iconic English rugby league player captained his Leeds Rhinos team to numerous victories, including seven Super League titles and two Challenge Cups. His exceptional kicking and tactical acumen made him one of the sport's greatest before he transitioned to rugby union as a player and then coach, helping Leicester Tigers to the Premiership before taking England to the 2023 World Cup semi-final. He is also widely celebrated for his fundraising efforts, notably raising millions for motor neurone disease (MND) research in honour of his former teammate Rob Burrow, who was diagnosed with MND.

His modus operandi is a simple – and immensely powerful – approach, learned as a callow ten-year-old boy. 'I was picked to represent Lancashire at under-nines,' he explained. 'I was a substitute and got on for the final two minutes.' Rather than feel pleased with his representative honour, it lit within him a competitive spark, which still burns brightly. 'After the game, I showered, got on the bus and remember thinking to myself, "I've drove all the way up here and played two minutes."' While his parents were 'chuffed to bits', it offered little satisfaction for Sinfield. He made a promise to himself. 'This isn't enough for me. Next year, when this team's picked, I'm going to be in it. I'm going to make sure I play from the start.'

However, this required a shift in perspective – in order to reach his goal, he needed to help others reach theirs. 'The following year, at the trials, you get split up into different teams and you're put with players from all clubs. I remember looking at my team thinking, *I am going to struggle to stand out and get in the side unless I can get the best out of those around me.*' His focus, then, was less on what he could do for himself and more on what he could do for his team. 'I spent the next forty-five minutes of this trial encouraging, pushing, driving, motivating every single one of these players in my team. We smashed everybody on that trial.'

'I am going to struggle to stand out and get in the side unless I can get the best out of those around me.' Kevin Sinfield

He was selected for Lancashire, spotted by Leeds and then selected at the age of sixteen to play in the club's first team. The rest is history.

To get the best out of those around me. Those nine words would shape the rest of his life. Sinfield's realisation of the importance of lifting others has defined his career – and is also grounded in robust science, which shows huge benefits both to teams and to individuals when focusing on getting the best out of one's peers.

Consider the last time you performed a tiny act of kindness for someone else. Now recall how you felt afterwards. Perhaps it was the quiet gratification of running errands for an elderly neighbour, or the sense of accomplishment you had after donating to a worthy charity. This 'warm glow' sensation, which frequently occurs after we engage in 'pro-social' conduct, is regarded to be one of the primary motivations of benevolent behaviour in humans.[1] We end up feeling more connected to other people, addressing one of our most basic psychological needs.[2]

Our brains are wired to do good. For instance, evidence from brain scans suggests a relationship between giving money to charity and the impact on our happiness. When we donate money to a good cause, it engages the same parts of the brain that are active when presented with financial incentives or sex. In fact, the mere thought of planning to behave with kindness and generosity may trigger changes in our brains that help us feel better.[3]

So everyone benefits when we seek to elevate the people around us – including the person doing the elevating. The question is how to do so.

As Kevin Sinfield found in his trial match, one method is to consistently offer positive verbal encouragement in order to help others fully realise their potential.

This was demonstrated in research conducted at Columbia University, in which participants were asked to share personal experiences about stressful life situations on online message boards and respond to other entries.[4] The participants spent three weeks offering each other alternative ways of seeing their situations, and sending kind words of support and acceptance. The findings indicated that supporting others in regulating their emotions predicted better emotional and psychological outcomes for the participants who received it.

So Sinfield's nine-word mantra worked. Better than that, though, it didn't just help his team – it helped Sinfield himself. And that makes sense. The research shows that when we help other people re-evaluate their challenges, it also affects the mood and subjective happiness of the encourager. High levels of self-focused attention is a common symptom of depression; the more people support others, it seems, the more their supportive actions help reduce their own low mood.

In other words, high performance depends less on trying to outperform others, and more on helping others on your way to the finish line. Following Kevin Sinfield's advice and being a more encouraging person means you will not only make yourself better liked, it will also make you like yourself better, too.[5]

WATCH
THE EPISODE

MARTIN LEWIS

TRUST COMES FIRST

Martin Lewis was sitting around a table with the bosses of the UK's big energy providers and the prime minister, David Cameron. They had a problem. 'Energy prices were going up and one of the bosses of the big energy firms said, "Prime Minister, we need your help",' Lewis said with a wry smile. '"People don't trust us. And therefore, we're not getting the information across that we need. We need your help. We need everybody in this room to help make sure that customers trust their energy firms."' Cameron nodded along in agreement.

'I put my hand up, and I was at the end of the room,' Lewis said. At first, he was ignored, but he persisted. 'Eventually, Cameron turned to me and he said, "Yes?"' Lewis steadied himself, and announced, 'I just want to say, having heard the call on trust, I will do everything I possibly can to ensure that *nobody* trusts you. Because you are not trustworthy.'

There was a moment of frosty silence, until Lewis explained his reasoning. 'The latest data shows 56 per cent, or whatever it was, of people who come to your call centres are given incorrect information.' He repeated his earlier claim. 'I will not tell people to trust you until you become trustworthy. You cannot market trust. Trust only comes from being trust*worthy*.'

Lewis would know. Over the last two decades, his name has become synonymous with trust. He is regularly cited as the most trustworthy man in the UK, while his company – MoneySavingExpert.com – is widely regarded as one of the UK's most trusted sources for personal finance and savings advice. What is his secret, we wondered?

'Trust only comes from a track record of doing the right thing or at least trying to do the right thing,' he explained. And it couldn't be more important: without trust, we are nothing. 'I once did a talk with some young entrepreneurs, just starting out, and someone asked me about "shortcuts".' His response was unequivocal. 'Woah, woah, woah, woah – stop, stop,' he shouted. 'Shortcuts might help a small business to be a bigger business, but if you want to be a big business and you've taken shortcuts, you're going to kill yourself in the future if you are throwing away that trust early. You have to be trustworthy from day one.'

He explained to us how he had set this standard in his own business. 'You have to do it right from the moment that you start,' he said, 'if you're setting out to be trustworthy. I have a massive professional paranoia to a ridiculous level that drives my team mad. It drives me mad.'

He recounted how this emphasis on not taking shortcuts had paid dividends. 'I want Money Saving Expert and the work I do to be trusted because that's my core belief,' he told us. 'That's what I believe, and that's why I do it. I also want to be very successful financially as well.'

This resolve was understood by everyone in his organisation. He recalled the words of a senior colleague who had recently joined the company from a big, very commercial employer. Lewis wondered whether he would want to focus on the bottom line of the company at the expense of the trustworthiness of its content – but he was wrong. 'He said, "Our biggest financial asset is the trust that people have in the site,"' Lewis recalled. '"We cannot do anything that breaches that." From his purely commercial perspective, for the longevity of the brand and the organisation, he came to the same conclusion as me,' he said. 'We had a shared aim even though we had entirely different belief sets which were driving us to it.'

Lewis's intuition about the importance of trust is well-founded. According to research, 55 per cent of CEOs consider a lack of trust a fundamental risk to their own organisations.[1] And within teams, we all have a sense that people work better when trust is the foundation upon which everything is built. In one comprehensive review of over 125 studies on this topic, researchers identified trust in teams as a crucial ingredient for increasing their performance and driving the happiness of its members.[2, 3] Those teams who have more trust actually perform better at tasks, have higher levels of team satisfaction, deeper relationship commitments and suffer less stress than when it is absent.[4] High levels of trust among team members has been found to encourage risk-taking and facilitate the sharing of knowledge and skills, leading to enhanced collaboration and productivity.[5]

So, how can we go about creating a sense of trust in any team or organisation? According to the psychologist Ron Friedman, it doesn't happen by accident. Based on his research, Friedman has five suggestions to enhance trust.[6] First, talking more. Friedman discovered that members of high-performing teams made an average of ten phone calls every day, compared to six on other teams.

Second, high-performing teams were more disciplined when it came to meetings, both in terms of planning for and attending them – everyone knows what to expect and what is expected of them.

Third, team members who were willing to share personal details about their life also developed high levels of trust with others: while it's tempting to believe that high-performing teams are solely focused on work and efficiency, they actually spend more time discussing non-work subjects and finding ways to connect in authentic ways. This in turn fosters, fourth, a culture in which it is simpler to express and receive greater gratitude. Many studies rank this higher on the list of things employees want, and Friedman says that 'when we share credit for our accomplishments, we appear more likeable without seeming any less capable.'[7]

Finally, Friedman discovered that when trust is present, both positive and negative emotions can be communicated more often. 'People can be celebrating successes but also expressing frustrations,' he observed. Friedman observes that when people's interactions are more authentic it creates a transparency that makes it easier to understand how they truly feel and where they stand.

MICRO-HABITS

Put in micro-habit terms? Well, it means more phone calls, having better meeting protocols, developing non-work-related relationships, increasing appreciation for others, and above all, encouraging people to be themselves at work. That sounds like a wonderful place to work.

WATCH
THE EPISODE

7

How to Build a Close-Knit Team

MICRO-HABITS

Your ego is your greatest enemy.

ANDY COLE

'WE' NOT 'ME'

In the early 1990s, during Andy Cole's time at Arsenal, Bristol City and then – to some acclaim – Newcastle United, his singular focus was on regularly finding the back of the net. It earned him an image of a lone gunslinger, solely focused on his own game and his goal tally. And yet in our conversation on the podcast, he was keen to emphasise that this was only the beginning of what he was about.

He recounted how, soon after joining Manchester United as a British transfer record signing, he was given an insight into what it takes to create success. The person who delivered the lesson was Brian Kidd, Sir Alex Ferguson's assistant and a celebrated former player in his own right. 'I remember Brian Kidd pulling me one day and saying to me, "Coley, if you think scoring forty goals at this football club is good enough, you're mad."' Cole smiled as he recalled his response. 'I remember looking at him and saying, "What are you on about? That's what it's about!"'

Kidd was unphased. 'It's more than one individual scoring forty goals and you running away celebrating while Manchester United finish second,' he told Cole. 'It's not about that. It's about you scoring goals to help your team win the Premier League or the FA Cup or whatever else we play in.'

With time, Cole came to understand the distinction being made. 'I think my time at Newcastle was all about me scoring goals. Everyone wanted me to score all the goals.' But things were different at Old Trafford. 'At Manchester United, we played as a team. The team ethic is what we do and what everyone must buy into.'

He paused and summarised the difference in two simple words. 'It's not about "I". It's about "us". That's it.' Once the penny had dropped, Cole realised that he had to change his thinking and adapt his approach. 'I had to build myself and integrate myself into the team to make myself a better player.'

This simple reframing – of changing your focus to home in on the shared, collective identity, at the expense of your own ego – is one that has been explored by the renowned psychologist Robert Cialdini. In fact, in a series of experiments, he demonstrated that within teams, your ego is your greatest enemy. He noticed that when people talk about their favourite sports team, they often choose one of two pronouns – 'we' or 'they'. What is especially interesting is how – and when – they are used.[1] Cialdini discovered that when discussing the team after a win, 'we' was the most commonly used term. 'We were amazing!' or 'We have a great striker.' However, when reflecting on a defeat, people aren't quite so keen to associate themselves with failure and instead employ the pronoun 'they'. 'They were really poor tonight.'

The psychologist dubbed this the BIRG and CORF effects: Basking In Reflected Glory, and Cutting Off Reflected Failure. We all want to be grouped with people and teams that do well and we want to put distance between ourselves and those that fail.

This tendency can have a pernicious impact. Psychologists Susan Gelman, Ariana Orvell and Ethan Kross have conducted fascinating experiments on children and adults. They provided them with almost identical versions of short stories involving a child who makes a small mistake and a teacher's response to it.[2] For example, a little girl dropped some stickers in a muddy puddle. In one version of the story, the teacher responded by focusing specifically on the child, saying 'Sometimes Sam drops things and she gets them yucky.' In another version, the teacher made a more general observation about people, saying 'Sometimes we drop things and we get them yucky.'

They consistently found that when a leader focuses on the individual – using words like 'you' and 'she' – it is dramatically more demotivating than when they focus on the group – using words like 'we'. 'When the teacher reframed the event by broadening the perspective, both children and adults judged the teacher as kinder, more tolerant of mistakes and more likely to help the child out by rectifying the mishap (for example, replacing the ruined items),' Gelman writes.[3] The psychologists suggest that talking about a challenging event with generalised pronouns – 'we need to stay together' – is a more effective way of bringing a group together and getting everyone to perform at their best.

Andy Cole would recognise this distinction, not least because of the effect it had on his trophy cabinet and the pleasure he derived from being part of such a collective endeavour. 'I enjoyed it all,' he said of his time at Manchester United. 'I enjoyed playing. I enjoyed the dressing room. Just being around all the boys and the team ethic.' He smiled, casting his mind back to the team that won the treble in 1999, and reiterated the alchemy that led to their success. 'It's not about me. It's about us.'

WATCH
THE EPISODE

CHRIS VOSS

SMALL TALK GETS BIG WINS

As the former chief hostage negotiator for the FBI, Chris Voss was used to being put in situations where hostages were trapped, emotions were running high and the odds of success were slowly diminishing. He understands how to build relationships founded on trust and focused on getting results.

So we wondered what huge, revelatory method he used to bring people together? His answer: small talk.

'Negotiation is the art of letting the other side have your way. How do you do that? You've got to let them talk.' He offered us an unexpected example: the world's most successful talk-show host. 'Oprah Winfrey might be the best negotiator on earth,' Voss said. 'Nobody thinks of her as a negotiator. Nobody. Yet Oprah has taken some highly volatile people to the woodshed over their misbehaviour and nobody knows about it, because of the way she handles it.' Voss pointed to her interview with disgraced cyclist Lance Armstrong. 'She said to him, "I'm going to put you on camera. I'm going to ask you a series of questions, bluntly asking you if you cheated and you're going to answer yes or no." He knew that going in and yet he still went on camera. That,' emphasised Voss, 'is a negotiation.'

> 'Negotiation is the art of letting the other side have your way.' Chris Voss

So, what can the rest of us learn from Oprah, we wondered? Above all, he says, to treat people with respect. 'The lasting impression the entertainment industry is infamous for is: "In in a limo, out in a taxi." With Oprah, you're "In in a limo, out in a limo,"' he said. 'Her overriding theme that they express, throughout her whole company, is no matter what happens, from beginning to end, everybody we deal with has to feel respected and well treated. No matter what the argument is, the last thing that Oprah says when she's finished is, "You have to understand that I will always love you and I will always support you."'

That is why small talk is so important, and not just under the bright lights of a television studio. It is a way of communicating mutual respect, which emphasises that both individuals can trust each other – Oprah-style. If you want somebody to trust you, maybe even like you, then you probably need to listen to their most inane chatter.

This is not mere conjecture. Indeed, one study from the University of Warwick suggests that engaging in just four minutes of small talk can help build trust. The researchers recruited over 300 people and separated them into two groups. Before meeting in person, each participant took a personality and IQ exam; the couple were then randomly selected to either have a four-minute text conversation or were not allowed to connect with their partner at all. They were then asked to guess features of their partner's personality, such as their level of extroversion, and forecast whether they would act collaboratively or selfishly in the two money-based games they were tasked to play.

Those who chatted fared better when they had to anticipate their partner's IQ and personality scores. However, they also tended to unconsciously ascribe and transfer their own personality traits on to their partner.

After that, the pairs got together in person and played a mental game called 'the public goods game'. In this game, each player was given twenty pounds and instructed to contribute to a shared pot of money with their partner. The psychologists found that those who had engaged in small talk with their partners before playing were more likely to correctly predict what they would share to the pot. What's more, those who had begun building a relationship through these conversations gave 30 per cent more than those who had not.[1]

This is an approach that Chris Voss would recognise. Small talk is the key to building positive relationships in every sphere of life, and that is a key ingredient of success. 'There isn't anybody in our life we don't have repeat relationships with,' Voss said. 'You go out and buy a car and you slaughter the dealer over the car price. If the car's a lemon, when you go back to that dealer they're not going to want to fix it. If the car is good, you go back to that dealer for routine maintenance, they're going to remember that you killed them before and they're not cutting you a break on anything. There's no such thing as a one-off.'

WATCH
THE EPISODE

JOE MARLER

EMOTIONAL GLUE

Joe Marler doesn't know what high performance is. Or so he told us.

'There's been occasions where I've felt I'm quite good at things,' England Rugby Union's talismanic forward was telling us. 'But then there's also been a lot of times where I'm really shit at things and I'm failing.'

It was an intriguing admission from one of England's most successful players. This was a man with ninety-five international caps who had won a Six Nations Grand Slam and played in a World Cup final – not to mention his celebrated two Premiership league titles with his team, Harlequins. We had a hunch that he might know more about high performance than he was letting on.

This self-deprecation led us to try a different tack. If he didn't know what high performance meant for him, perhaps he knew what it meant for the teams he had played in.

Upon hearing this revised question, Marler's eyes lit up. 'In successful teams, there always seems to be some sort of outside influence or emotional driver,' he said, animatedly. Without an 'emotional driver', any team is doomed to failure.

We wondered what form these 'drivers' tended to take. To Marler, it seemed to mean something beyond just the motive to win – a kind of emotional glue that bound a team together and transcended the simple desire to lift a trophy.

Joe had no shortage of examples. He invited us to consider South Africa, most recently world champions in 2019 and 2023 , who had used their racially diverse rugby team as a symbol of national pride in a country still grappling with the long shadows cast by apartheid. 'They wanted to win the World Cup, of course,' Marler said. 'But another big driver was actually uniting their country ... That's not specifically sport-related but it brings the team closer together and they go that extra mile.'

Or consider Saracens, the perennial champions. 'There was a big core of players that had grown up together through the academy and been through all sorts on and off the field.' But it wasn't just the team spirit that was binding them together. 'They were driven by a teammate, Henry Fraser,' Marler recalled. 'His brother was a teammate of theirs and he [Henry] had an accident and ended up being in a wheelchair. He's doing amazing things now but they became closer and tighter.'

Marler offered his own example, from when Harlequins won the Premiership in 2021. The team's head coach had been sacked halfway through the season. 'The senior players in the group were asking, "What's going to happen now?"'

In response, they found themselves reaching for a new kind of emotional glue, rooted in the desire of the players to transcend the chaos they were facing in the middle of the season. 'It accelerated them to go, "We've got to take charge and got to take more ownership here." In conjunction with the coaching staff, we had a player-led environment.

'That culture was brilliant, amazing,' Marler smiled. 'The players were in control. We got to dictate what we wanted to do in training. It turned into a more attack-based approach.' And it worked. In the semi-final, the team miraculously came back from 28–0 down at half-time to beat Bristol in overtime – only to then beat Exeter by two points in a nail-biting final.

Marler was clear: it is this sense of emotional connection that drives lasting success. 'It is the emotional bit . . . when you get it right, nails it and drives it. At the top level, everyone's pretty much on the same level physically. Everyone tends to have the same tactics. Everyone tends to have the same style of play. It's that emotional connection, how tight the group is, how hard they're willing to work for each other.'

We were particularly interested in Marler's argument because it corresponded with a growing range of evidence from psychological research. Social identity theory,[1] shows that people perform better when they feel a strong sense of belonging to a group with a shared identity. In elite sport, this identity can be emotionally charged and deeply symbolic, linking a team not just to victory but to something larger: their country, their history or a shared mission. Research highlights how performance under pressure improves when players feel they're not just playing *with* each other but *for* each other.

In one study, examining the emotional culture of teams working within a care home, the teams that expressed *companionate love* – that is affection, compassion, care and tenderness towards each other – outperformed those who didn't. The staff reported higher job satisfaction, better teamwork and significantly lower levels of burnout and absenteeism, while remarkably even the patients benefitted: they had better moods, fewer emergency visits and improved quality of life. The researchers concluded that emotional culture isn't soft or secondary: it's central to sustained high performance.[2]

And that's what Joe Marler was describing. In fact, he knows exactly what high performance is: when the emotional connection is strong, people go further, dig deeper and perform better. Not because they have to, but because they want to. Whether it's a rugby pitch, a hospital ward or any other environment that demands teamwork, that emotional glue – the sense that *we're in this together* – is what transforms performance from competent to exceptional.

WATCH
THE EPISODE

PIPPA GRANGE

THE TRIPLE H

Team building. These two words have the power to make eyes roll, arms cross and elicit a collective sigh from any organisation. Sure enough, some people find team-building exercises exciting – but more recoil in horror at the thought of this forced corporate fun/torture. Making time for such apparent triviality can feel like a waste of time.

But it doesn't have to be this way. Dr Pippa Grange, the renowned psychologist, is best known for her transformative work with elite athletes and teams – including England's national football squad – and has a different perspective on the concept.

'It's a defence of the fearful,' Pippa suggested of people who are intuitively sceptical of team-building exercises. 'It's like the people who don't feel that comfortable in their skin need a shield. Sometimes that shield is in making the other person feel more conforming or smaller or sharing the fear basically. That creates a shield but is really, really damaging.'

Any successful attempt at team building will, she says, first need to tackle that latent cynicism. 'In terms of performance, whether we're talking about that in an office setting or in a team setting, all that cynicism does is lower people's willingness to take a risk. And what does extreme elite performance require? Risk. You have to be vulnerable enough to put yourself out there.'

The question, then, is how to get people to feel comfortable taking on this risk – and to do so in front of their peers. To demonstrate how, Grange described an exercise that originated within the dressing room of NFL's Atlanta Falcons and was led by coach Mike Smith, who guided his team through one of the most striking turnarounds in NFL history. The concept was then adopted by Shane McCurry, a coach at Richmond Tigers, the Australian-rules football team where Grange had once worked. It's called: the Triple H exercise.[1]

'The Triple H exercise is being able to stand up and tell a story of a hero, hardship and highlight in your own life,' Grange explained. She told us how it was applied by the Aussie-rules giants. 'It's such a clean example of a turning point for them. The way that it's introduced is that it's an exercise in vulnerability. It's an exercise in getting to know each other so that the bond between the team is stronger. How do you really play for another person or support another person if you don't know them outside of their number or their role?'

In the fascinating book, *Yellow & Black: A Season with Richmond*,[2] the impact of this exercise is described in detail. 'There was not a single head in the room that wasn't solely focused on the person up the front, and it wasn't in a way that made them feel isolated,' the architect, Shane McCurry, says. 'It was that focus and that presence – that idea that "We're right here with you, we know you're doing it tough up there, but we're behind you."'

Tim Livingstone, the head of coaching at Richmond goes further. 'We're talking about stories of sickness and broken homes. Put it this way, if you've got to put your arse on the line for your mate, and take a hit on the field, you're more likely to do it if you have some care for what he's been through.'[3]

Grange agrees. 'The idea of a group, each taking a turn, over a season, to come to the front of the room with everybody sitting and listening and tell a story. The Triple H is just an anchor for the storytelling of the hero in your life, the hardship and the highlight, and almost everybody tells a personal story. That'll be about a grandma or a person who's meant everything to them, or a moment where they felt really small and overcame it. It's humbling. It really introduces humility.' And, in these expressions of humanity and vulnerability, the whole team comes together. 'The bond that comes out of doing that, like really seeing the person behind the shirt or the human being behind the role or the title is so rich,' Grange said.

At heart, it is this sense of vulnerability and risk-taking that distinguishes good teams from great ones. 'That's the

MICRO-HABITS

true question to the leader: Are you genuinely invested in the kind of culture that will enable your people to be vulnerable within that?' Grange told us. 'Will you manage your own fear to show up and do it every day?'

 **'Will you manage your own fear to show up and do it every day?'** Pippa Grange

This kind of vulnerability worked for England. In previous generations, club loyalties and egos had often divided the national team, but ahead of the 2018 World Cup, Grange's work helped tear down walls built on rivalry and replaced them with moments of connection. With that connection came a sense of freedom to express themselves, to take risks and to care about each other. On that occasion, Gareth Southgate's team went to the semi-finals, the furthest they had ventured since 1990, and would subsequently reach the final of the next two European Championships.[4]

As Pippa Grange emphasised, getting the most out of people means leaders and team members alike must be willing to be vulnerable. As a starting point, sharing your hero, hardship and highlight can be a quick and effective way of getting there – and reminding every member of the group that every other person they are with is truly human.

WATCH
THE EPISODE

8

How to Give (and Receive) Better Feedback

MICRO-HABITS

There is always common ground. A leader's job is to find it.

SARA DAVIES

RADICAL CANDOUR

'I'm big on family,' Sara Davies explained to us shortly after breezing into the *High Performance* studio. 'But the business isn't your family. Your family have to like you, they have to spend time with you, irrespective of what's going on in the rest of the world, right? The people who come to work do it because you pay them. It is a transactional relationship.'

A leading entrepreneur and investor on *Dragon's Den*, Davies learned this lesson many years ago after starting her first business, Crafter's Companion, while still an undergraduate at York University. 'I had a girl work for me who was employee number four,' Davies told us, smiling at the memories of her early days. 'When we were a small company she was in love with the company. It was brilliant. She used to go to trade shows with me and she'd bunk in, top and toe in the bed, because I could only afford a single room.

'As the business got bigger and we became, dare I say it, a little bit more corporate, I could see that this wasn't what she signed up for,' Davies said. 'It wasn't the sort of environment in which she flourishes, but because she loved me and she was connected with the business, she kept sticking it out.

'Eventually, she came into my office and said, "I'm really sorry, Sara. I handed my notice in to my boss today. I just wanted to tell you personally. I'm going to leave."'

Davies was overwhelmed by the news and started crying. 'She was like, "Oh my God. I knew you'd cry. I'm so sad."' But her colleague had misunderstood. 'I said, "I'm just so relieved. I'm so happy for you."'

Her colleague was confused. 'She said, "I thought you'd be devastated that I'm leaving." I said, "I am. You're going to be a huge loss to the company, but this company isn't right for you anymore. I have seen you sitting at your desk and you're not thriving. Ten years ago you used to thrive, and I can see it's not bringing you happiness. I'm so happy that you're going to move on to a business where you can feel that again."'

This exchange helped Davies recognise that sometimes honesty – even when it's hard – holds the key to the continued growth of her team and her business. 'It's so difficult to have these conversations with people,' she conceded. But it's also deeply necessary.

What was the secret, we asked her? 'Are you familiar with *Radical Candor*?'[1] she asked, referencing the book by Kim Scott, a former Apple and Google executive. In her book, Scott defines the term 'radical candor' as 'feedback that incorporates both praise and criticism.'

'It's a principle I follow in my everyday life,' Davies told us. 'People only ever get better if they are constantly in pursuit of feedback and constructive criticism to keep improving. For a lot of my senior staff ... that I coach, it's all about giving them feedback to make them better.'

 **'People only ever get better if they are constantly in pursuit of feedback.'** Sara Davies

This skill wasn't something that came readily to her. 'Someone once said to me, "How do you give feedback?" And I said, "Oh, I'm brilliant at it. I use 'the shit sandwich' method" – that is, one piece of praise, one piece of criticism, another piece of praise. The problem was, I delivering a wafer-thin slice of ham in a big fat loaf of bread,' she laughed. The praise was drowning out the criticism – to the detriment of her team.

One day, her colleague offered her a different metaphor. 'What was needed was a steak in a pitta,' she said. 'This is the concept of "radical candour". It's all about when you give feedback, it's about caring humanly, really caring about somebody deeply but being very direct.'

She expanded on this food theme. 'When you talk to people, if you flower it up, if you put the pitta around the steak, it's just a load of waffly bullshit ... The more that you give this fluff, the more insincere you feel and people don't trust you.' Instead, her approach is more direct. 'I've learned to strip back all of the fluff, all of the insincerity and just show people that I care about them deeply. As difficult as it is for me to give them this feedback, I'm doing it so that they can get better and progress in their career, in their job and in their business.'

This is a defining skill. 'This is what's changed me from being a successful entrepreneur to a *really* successful entrepreneur.'

Davies isn't the only one to have taken inspiration from this method. In her book, Kim Scott explains how she has helped teams achieve a 'bullshit-free' environment by understanding the four different styles of feedback that are commonly used. These are: manipulative insincerity, obnoxious aggression, ruinous empathy and, finally, radical candour. Like Sara Davies acknowledged, understanding which one you are prone to using can help you adapt and deliver feedback that counts.

'People give praise and criticism that is manipulatively insincere when they are too focused on being liked or think they can gain some sort of political advantage by being fake,' Scott writes. Meanwhile, obnoxious aggression is a style that belittles others, embarrasses them, or leaves them feeling frozen out. 'It sometimes gets great results short-term but leaves a trail of dead bodies in its wake in the long run,' suggests the author.

Ruinous empathy, meanwhile, is the most common type of feedback. It involves sugar-coating the messages in an attempt to make them land better, yet it often dilutes the main message and then undermines the feedback. Finally, Scott explains that 'radical candour' is the sweet spot between caring about your team but directly challenging them too. 'Candid feedback is offered humbly. Implicit with candour is that you're simply offering your view of what's going on and that you expect people to offer theirs. If it turns out that in fact you're the one who got it wrong, you want to know.'

Scott argues that when people trust you and believe

you care about them, the effects are myriad. They tend to accept – and act on – your praise and criticism; they tell you what they really think about what you are doing well and, more importantly, not doing so well. And it works. A 2017 study published in the *Academy of Management Journal* found that constructive, direct feedback leads to better learning and performance outcomes than indirect or sugar-coated feedback.[2] Other research indicates that employees who receive frequent, honest feedback are 3.5 times more likely to be engaged at work.[3]

This is something that Davies knows better than anyone. She explained to us what happened after she had her candid conversation with her erstwhile colleague about why it was good for her to leave. 'She didn't leave to go to another business,' she beamed. 'She left and set up her own small business using the skills that she'd learned working with me for all those years. She is thriving again.'

WATCH
THE EPISODE

JORDAN HENDERSON

DEALING WITH DISSENTERS

When Jürgen Klopp first arrived at Liverpool, he tried to change the team's training times. 'For most of our career we would train in the morning,' Jordan Henderson, Liverpool's captain and Klopp's right-hand man, explained to us on the podcast. 'We would come for 9.30 a.m., train at eleven.' Klopp believed that if the team were playing a match in the evening, training should replicate this and begin late in the afternoon. 'It would get the body ready for that time of playing, which, when you think about, makes sense,' his captain surmised.

What was the reaction, we asked? Moaning. 'The lads were coming in and felt a bit lethargic and a bit tired,' Henderson said. 'It's getting dark, you're going out, the floodlights are on. A few of the lads pulled me aside and said, "Could we not have it earlier?" As captain, I felt as though I needed to at least ask the question.'

Henderson described knocking on his manager's door to recount the discussion. '"Gaffer," I said, "a few of the lads are struggling with these later training times. They feel a bit tired. Is there any way we could train in the morning?"' Klopp responded with curiosity. 'He looked at me and asked, "Who has said that? Who is moaning about it?"' Henderson was keen not to reveal the names: 'I can't say any names. I can't be chucking people under the bus.' Instead, he spoke in vague terms. 'I said, "There's quite a few and that's why I've come. There's quite a few that want earlier training."'

After some consideration, Klopp asked Henderson to pass on an invitation to his teammates: 'Tell them, if anybody's got an issue with the training time, to come and tell me and speak to me directly.' Henderson did his duty. 'I've walked out and gone back to the lads and said, "If you want it that badly, just go and speak with him yourself."'

How many members of the dressing room accepted the invitation to meet with the leader? 'No one. No one ever went up,' was Henderson's reply.

This anecdote contains an important lesson on how the best leaders respond to one of our favourite pastimes: moaning. One study discovered that we grumble an average of eleven times every day, with three of those grumbles occurring before we even get out of the house. Another study found that we complain to others for up to twenty minutes each day, which is more than seventy-seven hours a year.[1] On weekends, we increase our griping, up to sixteen times a day.[2]

As it turns out, moaning is far more exhausting than being positive. A month-long study by Michigan State University discovered that employees who complain are more mentally fatigued than those who have a positive outlook. 'The constant state of vigilance is depleting,' the report found.

Interestingly, whining increases when we try to bond with a colleague. One study discovered that groups working on a project together groaned fifty times in an hour, equivalent to nearly one complaint every eighty seconds.[3]

As Klopp intuitively understood, the links forged by moaning can be powerful – but also unhealthy. Psychologist Jeffrey Lohr of the University of Arkansas explains it like this: 'People don't break wind in elevators more than they have to. Venting anger is ... similar to emotional farting in a closed area.'[4] Why? Because chronic complainers have a negative impact on others around them. When people think and respond negatively and pessimistically, they unintentionally transmit their thoughts on to others in a process known as 'projective identification'.[5] Melanie Klein, a psychoanalyst, initially described this concept in the 1940s. It involves an individual unknowingly projecting their emotions on to another, and if accepted, both parties end up feeling the same way. Part of our evolutionary nature is this form of 'transfer' – in which a bad mood spreads from one person, to another, to the whole group.[6]

As social animals, our brains unconsciously take on the emotions of those around us. And this can have a risky side, as Jürgen Klopp understood. People that moan about everything can become contagious. Before we know it, we find ourselves moaning too.

So what should high performers do to minimise the risk of perpetual moaning? First, take a page from Klopp's book: don't ignore the complaints, but don't indulge them either. Instead, invite accountability by asking people to speak up directly if it matters that much to them. As Henderson found from his teammates' reluctance to speak to the manager themselves, more often than not the noise fades when responsibility is required.

Secondly, steer the energy. When moaning starts, be ready to greet it with a calm curiosity and ask: 'What do you want to be different?' This simple question helps shift the spotlight from a sense of helplessness to a call to action. As Klopp and Henderson showed, in high-performing cultures, dissatisfaction isn't silenced but redirected.

WATCH
THE EPISODE

GORDON RAMSAY

DON'T TAKE IT SO PERSONALLY

'This fish is so *raw* he's still finding Nemo.'

'There's enough garlic in here to kill every vampire in Europe.'

'You used so much oil the US want to invade the fucking plate.'

'This lamb is so undercooked it's following Mary to school.'

'Why did the chicken cross the road? Because you didn't fucking cook it!'

When you type the words 'Gordon Ramsay feedback' into an internet search engine, you are greeted by a tsunami of entertaining insults. So, you can imagine why we were a little daunted to meet the acclaimed chef on the podcast. We soon found out, however, that there was a deliberate strategy underlying his feedback.

'You need to be a sponge. The best listening device is you,' he told us. 'But take it professionally, not personally. Getting told off is fucking good. It's really healthy.'

Ramsay's belief in the importance of harsh feedback is rooted in his own experiences, which took him from failed footballer to one of the best chefs on the planet. 'You've got to have thick skin,' he told us. 'And you've got to live in the real world.'

'You've got to have thick skin. And you've got to live in the real world.' Gordon Ramsay

The trick, he said, was to keep on getting feedback – and to keep on learning. He worked with some of the best in the industry. 'I had father figures in my life. Marco Pierre White was like a big brother/father figure. Albert Roux at Le Gavroche was another father figure. Guy Savoy in Paris.'

With each of them, he would constantly seek out their opinion on his work. 'I was on a pursuit to garner all this info,' he said. 'Intel, intel, everywhere I went, give me the intel. What is it? How does that sourdough work perfectly? How do you bone out a pigeon beautifully and not waste anything on that carcass? And so that intel was this gathering of incredible stuff.'

How can each of us become better at receiving feedback to be able to do our own incredible stuff? After all, most feedback *doesn't* get taken on board. In one review of hundreds of feedback experiments, dating back to 1905, scientists found that in 38 per cent of cases, feedback – even when it was positive – not only did not improve performance, it actively made it worse.[1]

So, how do we adopt Ramsay's advice and learn to be

a 'sponge' with a 'thick skin'? One answer comes from the organisational scientists Avraham Kluger and Dina Nir, who propose what they call 'feedforward'. As the name implies, feed*back* tends to focus on past performance and what you should have done. Feed*forward* discussions focus on what you will do. They encourage you to understand how to improve future performance.

In one study of this approach, one group of employees were given a normal appraisal by their managers and the other half had a feedforward discussion instead. Four months later, those who were given feedforward advice were found to be performing significantly better than their colleagues given the traditional appraisal.[2]

When viewed from this perspective, Ramsay's success in the kitchen and in the boardroom of his business empire seems to be less about his relentless appetite for proving himself right and more about his willingness to understand where he had gone wrong so he could continue to get better at his craft.

WATCH
THE EPISODE

DAME LAURA KENNY

DISAGREE AGREEABLY

Laura Kenny is the most successful British female Olympian. With five Gold medals to her name, she reigned supreme in the velodrome for three cycles of the Olympic calendar. So we were surprised to learn that she doesn't believe her success is down to her athleticism, or even her work ethic. She attributes her success to her communication style.

'I always say my best tool and the tool that I've used throughout my career is talking,' she told us. 'I think that has helped me to be as successful as I am. I've never been scared to raise my hand and ask a stupid question or say if I don't agree with something. I just think I've always been quite good at it.'

It was an intriguing argument. After all, cycling – even team cycling – is not always seen as a sport that depends on effective communication. Isn't the trick just to pedal faster than everyone else? But Kenny gave us an example to demonstrate that in the velodrome, effective communication is make or break.

She described the lead-up to the 2016 Rio Olympic Games when Team GB's final line-up was about to be decided. After years of training and dedication, this moment was make or break. Tensions were rife, and communication completely broke down. 'Some of the ways that people were communicating at the time was savage,' Kenny recalled. 'I didn't agree with the language that was being used.

'When you are in the team pursuit line, you can shout what you want really, but we always use [terms] like "hold" "squeeze" or "change" if you think someone needs to get out of the way. But it started to get a little bit abusive. It was getting intense because people were wanting to be selected for the bike races. There were a couple of times where people would be doing things to screw someone else over.' She shook her head at the memory of teammates eagerly seizing upon others' mistakes and failures.

Kenny felt obliged to act. 'I remember coming off the track and being like, "No. We are not talking like that. We're a team going for gold medals. We are not talking like that. I'm sorry. I'm not having swearing – and I swear quite a lot, but when it comes to a bike race, I'm not having people getting called rude names."' She enlisted the team psychologist Steve Peters for an intervention and eventually, she won out. The swearing stopped – and the outcomes of the team improved.

We asked Kenny for some examples of her personal approach to communication. She described the way she resolves conflicts with husband Jason – a fellow gold medallist with whom Kenny had first struck up a relationship after the London Olympics. They used to argue a lot, she told us. 'When it comes to an argument with Jason, because I know it winds him up, I just stop talking. And it will go on for a day, and we wouldn't have spoken because he'll be wanting to argue and I'm not,' she said. 'It got to a point where it wasn't really productive.'

But in time, the couple began to discuss how to overcome their differences. 'We agreed that he wouldn't go mental, and I would open up and actually say what the issue was.' This hasn't stopped them having disagreements, but it has made them more adept at resolving them. 'Yes, we still argue, but it isn't like one person just getting their point across and the other one just ignoring them. We have got to a point where we meet in the middle on how we want to resolve our issues.'

Kenny may not have known it, but her approach – finding the common ground and going from there – is increasingly seen as the best way to end conflict within groups. There is always common ground. A leader's job is to find it. In one study conducted at Yale University, two sets of people were asked to debate highly emotional themes in an online chatroom. Before starting, each group received a unique set of instructions. Group One was instructed to adopt a competitive mindset in order to 'win' the debate. Group Two was instructed to 'argue to learn', meaning they should try to get a deeper grasp of a specific problem rather than a battle of wits to be won. In the study, those who 'argued to win' tended to take a firm position and only saw one correct solution. Those who argued to learn displayed greater flexibility of thought and were more likely to accept opposing viewpoints.[1] It's this flexibility that gives people the space to reach a healthy compromise.

MICRO-HABITS

Laura Kenny's approach to arguing effectively offers profound insights for developing the connections found in high-performing teams. Her insistence on respectful communication and psychological safety is pivotal in fostering a productive team environment. Although it might not feel like it, learning how to argue with your team makes you work better together.

**WATCH
THE EPISODE**

9

How to Perform Under Pressure

MICRO-HABITS

You can never eliminate fear. But you can learn to look it in the eye.

STEVE PETERS

'WHAT IF . . . ?'

When we met with Professor Steve Peters, the forensic psychiatrist whose advice helped turned British Cycling into a medal factory without parallel, he regaled us with tales of his menagerie in the Derbyshire countryside where he houses rescued animals. 'I've got a massive interest in animal rescue,' he explained to us. 'I've got donkeys, chickens, dogs, horses . . .' he began to list them all. 'I also do people rescue,' he added, almost as an afterthought.

While we enjoyed his obvious passion for helping distressed creatures, we were keen to focus on the animal with which he has become synonymous: the chimp. Well before meeting Peters, we had come across his work through the insights of Sir Chris Hoy and Jordan Henderson, both of whom had adopted his invaluable way of keeping calm under pressure.

It was rooted in his distinction between the impulsive 'chimp brain' and the rational 'human brain'.[1] The chimp brain evolved first, and deals with deep-rooted emotional reactions – it reacts only to drives and instincts, which you experience as involuntary emotions like fear, anger, hunger. On the other hand, the 'human' part of our brain – the neocortex – is responsible for all voluntary movements and our interpretations of sensory data, plus all the 'higher' functions from speech and reasoning to abstract thought and a social conscience.

Peters was happy to tell us about how we could use this distinction too. The most effective way to perform under pressure, he said, is to learn how to get your chimp brain under the control of your human brain. 'If someone's in a good place, *nothing* touches them,' he began. 'If someone's not in a good place, *anything* can touch them . . . If I can show you how to run your mind, nothing's going to touch you.'

'If I can show you how to run your mind, nothing's going to touch you.' Steve Peters

He concedes that this isn't necessarily easy to achieve. 'It's a skill that has to be worked on. It's a bit like getting fit. You've got to keep practising every day.' We can all learn to better control our emotions by asking ourselves a series of simple questions on a regular basis.

First, you need to identify if your chimp brain is being too dominant. Ask yourself, 'Do I want to think or feel like this?' If the answer is no ('nearly everyone says no,' says Peters) then that means your chimp brain is in charge.

At that point, we need to quickly pivot to the second question: What's my plan? This is a quick-fire way to put your human brain back in the driver's seat. Even if we do not immediately know the answer, it causes a massive shift. Peters told us a story to illustrate the point. He picked some apples in the wilds and took them to a conference he was giving. 'I asked [people] to juggle ... Everyone could do two apples but most people couldn't do three, and nobody managed four.'

Peters' impromptu circus-skills training had a powerful point. 'That's how your mind works,' he said. 'Once you've got more than two problems, your mind's going to start stressing and going round and round.' But when we try to come up with a strategy, we shift from those unhelpful chimp-like emotions to the human part of the brain that craves logic and reason. 'Once we put things down and say, "There's six things we're going to address," there's a sense of relief because now we have a plan, which is what the brain is looking for.'

Sometimes, these two questions are enough to make you reset. But it is Peters' third and final question that is the most powerful way of all to deal with high-pressured moments: 'What if ... ?'

Peters describes that, tucked away in a corner of your brain, is a nifty little button that generates all the potential outcomes of an event. In theory, this 'What if?' button is there to protect you from danger. However, both your human brain and chimp brain can use, and sometimes abuse, it. 'Your chimp,' he says, will 'use it emotionally. It will ask questions like: What if I fail my GCSEs? What if I fail my driving test? What if my partner leaves me?'

The chimp part of our brain asks these distressing questions because it can't reason, leaving your mind to spiral.

For example, imagine you are running late to an important meeting, but you get stuck in traffic. Your chimp will ask, 'What if I'm late? What if I get in trouble?' Before you know it, road rage starts to roar inside of you. But Peters says this rage comes from your chimp's unrealistic expectations. 'It says, "I want the traffic to flow smoothly, no one to jump in, no one to cut me up." It is so ridiculous,' he laughed, 'There are always going to be idiots on the road or people having a bad day or people making mistakes. Our chimps don't interpret any of that.'

If we choose to engage the human brain, we can start by thinking of the 'What if?' scenarios and planning accordingly. 'You can then set off in a different mode by saying, "There will be idiots, there'll be people who make mistakes and there are people who might regret what they've done."'

These questions, he suggests, are key to resilience and robustness. 'They can get you in a good place and show you how to run your mind, so nothing's going to touch you. The kids won't touch you for being late to school because you'll deal with it. Someone cuts you up, you won't have road rage. In fact, nothing's going to get to you,' he promised. 'Now, I'm not wanting people to be robots. But I'm saying you'll manage any feeling you get, but generally most of the negative emotions won't appear. They just don't happen.'

There is plenty of evidence that Peters' 'What if?' question has remarkable evidence. The psychology writer Gary Klein[2] cites one study,[3] where it was found that prospective hindsight – that is, imagining that an event has already occurred – increases the ability to correctly identify reasons for how an event will actually unfold by 30 per cent. Klein

'WHAT IF . . . ?'

used this initial insight to devise a method which he called a *pre-mortem*, where teams identify potentially terminal risks to their plans before they take action.

Klein suggests that beginning with the 'What If?' question, of assuming the 'patient' has died, and then asking what *did* go wrong, the team members are then able to generate plausible reasons for the project's failure. 'A pre-mortem may be the best way to circumvent any need for a painful post-mortem,' suggests Klein. We suspect Steve Peters would agree.

Sometimes, asking 'What if?' is the best way to stop the 'if' happening in the first place.

WATCH
THE EPISODE

FERNANDO ALONSO

GAME FACE

Before he came into the room, Fernando Alonso had told his colleagues that he would see how long he could answer our questions with single-word answers. We had high hopes for this challenge. After all, this is a man whose steely determination behind the wheel has, since he started driving at the age of three, turned him into one of the greatest F1 drivers to have ever lived. On the podcast, his resolve was not as long-lasting as we might have predicted. Approximately thirty seconds, as it turned out.

Nevertheless, we still wondered how he was able to 'switch on' – mentally and physically – in the moments that mattered. Having won thirty-two Grands Prix since his F1 debut in 2001, he seemed to know exactly how to get himself into a winning mindset. His answer was quite unlike anything we had expected.

'It's about executing the race as a robot,' he explained. 'No emotion and only one way – to see the chequered flag faster than any other.' What did he mean, we wondered?

'When I close the visor, I remember everything that I spoke about with the team: each of the areas that are important in terms of performance: the engine, the tyres, aerodynamics and strategy,' he explained. 'I tried to deliver what they told me in the most efficient way. I take responsibility to deliver that job and be the last [link in the] chain.'

It's easy to think that this approach amounts to little more than taking things slightly too seriously. But research from the University of Tennessee would suggest there is something to it. In one study, Matthew Richesin and his team of psychologists explored whether a 'game face' – defined as a 'serious, focused or determined facial expression,' like Alonso's robotic mask – could help people perform better when completing tasks such as solving complex puzzles.

Before starting the exercises, the participants were shown pictures of athletes and other celebrities wearing a game face. Think of Portuguese footballer Cristiano Ronaldo's 'power pose' before he strikes a winning free kick, or swimming legend Michael Phelps' angry glare prior to winning one of his twenty-three gold medals. Each participant was then asked to adopt a similar 'look of intense determination'.

The participants were then given the job of putting together as much of a 100-piece puzzle as they could in a period of five minutes. One group was told to play with their 'game face' on, while the others were given no such instruction. The difference was stark. The group that was playing with their game faces on performed, on average, 20 per cent better than the control group – and also demonstrated better stress recovery.

Even Alonso is human, though. Was he always successful

in putting on his game face, we wondered? 'When you are racing, there is high adrenaline and moments when you are very emotional,' he laughed. 'I'm still a human being and very enthusiastic about what we are doing. That's the beauty of the sport. Even if you want to do something with no emotion, everything comes alive in certain moments of the race.'

WATCH
THE EPISODE

ALEX HONNOLD

EMBRACE THE FEAR

What happens if you fall down the most formidable rock-climb in the world?

'On El Cap, you don't just fall,' Alex Honnold told us. 'You rag-doll down the wall, because most of it is less than vertical. You're only going to fall thirty metres until you bounce off this ledge where you'll break both your legs and, hopefully, pass out.

'Then it's all disaster from there. You're going to explode like a water balloon at the base after bouncing off a bunch of things.' He noted the look of horror which passed across our faces with a look of faint amusement. 'It's horrible,' he concluded.

He would know. Alex Honnold is not just a rock climber. Lithe, laconic and laid-back, he is the living embodiment of what it means to push human limits. We met him in Las Vegas, his home base in the Nevada desert, where he has plotted and planned some of climbing's most breathtaking free-solo ascents – most famously his historic, rope-free climb of Yosemite's indomitable El Capitan.

His feats are so extreme that scientists have studied his brain, uncovering that his amygdala – the part responsible for fear – barely reacts to situations that would terrify most people. Where did this come from, we asked him? He was keen to stress that it wasn't a condition he was born with – it was something he had developed through a combination of discipline, preparation and an intimate understanding of risk.

Honnold explained how he had spent ten years visiting the mountain before his famous climb. In his sixth year of standing at the base and looking up at the 7,573-foot face, he finally conceded that 'it's never going to look easy. It's really scary. Just thinking about it would make your stomach turn a little bit.

'I think people watch the film and they're like, "There's something wrong with your brain,"' he smiled. 'No. It's probably the ten years of being scared all the time that has desensitised me to a point that I don't show any signs of it.'

He began applying his own version of a common treatment that dates back to the early 1900s: exposure therapy. When you're scared of an object or activity, a common coping technique is to simply avoid it. If you are afraid of enclosed spaces, for instance, you may avoid taking the lift. If you feel sick at the idea of talking in public, you sit as far back in the room as possible. If you are planning on climbing El Capitan without a rope, you spend years convincing yourself that it's impossible. While this may help you feel better in the short term, it can cause both fear and anxiety to worsen in the long term.[1]

Exposure therapy is a method that helps break the fear-avoidance cycle by exposing you to the source of your fear in an environment in which you know it can't harm you. If you can learn to deal with it in a safe context, perhaps you can learn to deal with it in a more dangerous one too.

This approach was first pioneered in the 1960s by Victor Meyer, a psychologist who had seen it work with frightened animals: exposed to a fearful object in captivity, the animals eventually exhibited reduced levels of fear around it at all times. He reasoned this could be applied to people and tried it with two patients suffering from OCD. He exposed them to objects that triggered their anxiety while preventing them from carrying out their usual compulsions. The treatment proved successful enough to spark wide interest among the therapist community.[2] Today, exposure therapy is used to address a host of psychological disorders, including phobias, panic disorder and PTSD.[3]

Honnold recognised this approach. 'When was the last time most people were actually afraid?' he asked. 'When's the last time people faced actual fear? I suspect that most people working in a city, working in office, don't experience real fear that often.' Facing fears, he argues, is essential. 'There's something useful to it. In some ways, it keeps the rest of your life more grounded. If you don't experience real fear from time to time then your mind creates fears out of nothing.' He offers an example from his travels. 'When I'm in airports, I always hear people stressing. "What do we do here? What if we miss the flight?" You're in a climate-controlled airport. There's food everywhere. There's abundance all around you. How could you get so worked up about things that do not matter?

MICRO-HABITS

'The more experiences you have with real fear, the less likely you are to make mountains out of molehills and worry about the stuff that doesn't matter,' he reasons.

 'The more experiences you have with real fear, the less likely you are to make mountains out of molehills.' Alex Honnold

What does this 'immersion treatment' look like in practice, we wondered? Most of us are not Honnold. That means you can never eliminate fear. But you can learn to look it in the eye. Honnold suggests starting with taking small steps to reduce your anxiety. Take gearing up to climb a huge mountain. 'The first time, you stand next to the plane. The next time, you walk up the steps, but then you turn around and walk back. That's the thing with climbing. It's really easy to steadily push your experience. You can always do something a little bit harder, a little bit bigger, a little bit more wild, a little bit different.

'It's really easy to turn up the dial with fear,' he expands. 'You know, it wasn't scary last time, but this time it's a little scary and then next time it's a little scarier. Eventually,' he laughs, 'you're doing things that seem totally insane.'

WATCH
THE EPISODE

GRAHAM POTTER

NO COMFORT ZONES

Graham Potter found himself unemployed on his wedding day.

'I got married on the same day that it was announced I was being released from York ... which was nice,' he once explained. 'My first dance with my wife after getting married was, "By the way, I'm unemployed!"'[1]

He had started his football career a few years earlier, identified as a teenage prodigy by his hometown club Birmingham City before moving to Stoke City and then on to Southampton. But he soon found himself losing altitude, and was released by the club before beginning his descent down the football pyramid, eventually arriving at York City in the fourth tier. So, after marrying Rachel, he tried something new. He started his coaching journey at Leeds Metropolitan and Hull universities, studying emotional intelligence while practising it on the football field.

By the time he moved to northern Sweden to assume control of Östersunds FK, a small team in the country's fourth tier, his distinctive approach was well established. Over the next seven years he took them to the top division, winning trophies at home and impressing in Europe. He would go on to take over Swansea and then Brighton, who he took to its highest ever Premier League finishes over three seasons.

We were speaking to Potter shortly after his most dramatic turn yet. He had answered a call from Todd Boehly, the new owner of Chelsea, who had offered him a five-year contract – only to change his mind seven months later, leading to Potter's dismissal. And yet it wasn't getting him down. Why? Because the trick to success, he said, is learning to manage discomfort.

'People in football talk about wanting to develop not just the footballer but the person,' he explained to us. 'A lot of it was about how you can make people uncomfortable but be comfortable in the uncomfortable situation.' Potter understood that to achieve this objective there were some important factors to address, not least being willing to lead the way and take part in the ballet himself. 'Take away the blame. Take away the hierarchy within the team,' he reasoned. This way, he helped his team to understand that they were all facing the same fears. 'Everyone's the same. Everyone's scared. Everyone's worried about bloody doing *Swan Lake* in front of people,' he smiled.

⚡ **'Take away the blame.'** Graham Potter

This was not, we discovered, a metaphor. Potter had literally got his Swedish team to perform Tchaikovsky's *Swan Lake*. 'You need a high-trust environment to be able to do something like that,' he told us. Not everyone was convinced by that strategy. 'When we started it, we weren't doing so well, so people are initially going, "Maybe it's because you're dicking around doing all this stuff. It's the reason why you're not winning. Why are you wasting your time rehearsing for a play?"'

Internally, however, Potter was sure of the benefits of performing the ballet. He also opened the evening by singing the regional Jämtland anthem in front of 3,000 intrigued locals ('I was terrible,' he recalled). 'This is part of how we created our own identity,' he said. 'How we created something for these players to come up to the northern part of Sweden.' As well as stretching their comfort zone, the experience also coincided with improved on-field performances. 'Along the way we had results and all of a sudden there was a story developing, a narrative developing that this is different, this is good and this is part of who we are.' The benefits of this experience eventually manifested itself in sustained on-field success in Sweden and European competition.

Educational theorist Tom Senninger describes this as the 'Learning Zone Model',[2] where human development sits between two extremes: the comfort zone, where things feel easy but nothing changes, and the panic zone, where fear overwhelms and learning becomes impossible. The sweet spot is the learning zone – a space of challenge, uncertainty and emotional stretch. It's here that resilience is formed, creativity unlocked and strength of character forged. The key is staying long enough in this space to understand and control your response to pressure without tipping into panic.

It worked for Potter. After countless ballet performances,

his team reached their very first Swedish cup final. He wanted to remind them of their qualities and the hurdles they had overcome to reach this far. 'I wrote a letter to the parents to say, "Thank you. Your son has contributed [to our success]. It'd be quite nice if you could write something back to them, just to explain how proud you are of them and what they've achieved. What they're doing now is really special and we're really grateful."'

The effect from the parental responses he received was significant. 'It was just this powerful moment,' Potter recounted. 'They're opening and they're reading the letter from their parents about how much they love them and how proud they are.' It was another reminder of the benefits of being willing to embrace the unknown.

WATCH
THE EPISODE

10

How to Do the Work

MICRO-HABITS

Hard work is the rocket fuel of high performance.

MARO ITOJE

THE SHIT PEOPLE DON'T SEE

When Maro Itoje walked into the *High Performance* studio, he immediately left both of us feeling distinctly underdressed. His tailored shirt, his elegant blazer and his well-polished shoes gave us a clear indication that this was a man who prided himself on paying attention to the smallest of details.

During our conversation it became ever clearer why he paid so much attention to these seemingly small things. He has built a career – and a gold-plated reputation – on focusing on them.

As soon as we began our discussion with the Saracens and England rugby player he was eager to explain an initialism that he and his teammates have stitched into the fabric of their club's jersey: TSPDS. Or: The Shit People Don't See.

'TSPDS: it's about all the little things that make a winning team that the outside world doesn't necessarily pay too much attention to,' Itoje said. 'Without that, the star moments can't happen.

'As with most things in life, you always see the highlight moments and the big landmark moments, which capture everyone's imagination,' he said. 'It's more than likely there's loads of little things that have happened in the background that have allowed that [particular] moment to take place.' In the Saracens culture, in which he has been nurtured since joining their youth team at the age of fourteen, TSPDS has an almost sacred quality.

He offered us some example of how Saracens pay 'significant attention' to the people doing the stuff that people don't see. 'It could be a kick chase. It could be getting up from the ground quickly and getting back in the line. It could be just making extra effort to put pressure on the opponent's foot so his kick is 5 per cent worse than what it would have been,' he said, counting on his hand. 'It could be anything really – but all those little things make a big difference.'

He lowered his voice to hammer his point home: 'One of my coaches told me once that nothing is ever neutral. You're either positively influencing the team or you're negatively influencing the team. No action is neutral. Everything you do matters.' Hidden hard work is the rocket fuel of high performance.

⚡ 'Everything you do matters.' Maro Itoje

In focusing on these small, transformative actions, Itoje was reflecting one of the most notable findings from recent psychological research. His hard-won wisdom is echoed in research conducted by Roy Baumeister, who was especially interested in how praising certain behaviours and actions can enhance or erode – or to quote Itoje, 'move you towards or away from' your own performance levels.

In a series of experiments,[1] Baumeister and his colleagues discovered that when an individual was praised for a good performance on any task that is difficult and requires skill and experience, it actually increased the chances of them delivering a poorer performance on the next task of a similar kind. It seems that praising someone for a skill, which is done automatically, creates a surge of self-awareness. This then breaks their natural flow, disrupting the smooth execution of well-honed skills.

But the opposite was true of what Baumeister called 'effortful tasks': tasks that require some effort but no skill or experience. These are the tasks that many in the rugby world christen 'TNTs' – Takes No Talent. When these were praised, it tended to have a positive effect on subsequent performance levels because it draws their attention to something they may not even realise they are doing and so increases the likelihood of them doing it again.

If we revisit the list of tasks which Itoje recounted when defining TSPDS – a kick chase, getting up from the ground quickly and getting back in the line, investing an extra effort to put pressure on an opponent – it's notable what he omits. Each one is an effortful task rather than a skill-based one, like a spectacular pass, a pinpoint kick or a dazzling try. By focusing on the small, easy steps – rather than the large, overwhelming ones – you can accomplish true and lasting success.

Itoje understood the comparison immediately. 'At Saracens, effort errors aren't acceptable,' he told us. 'If you make a skill error, then we can work on that. But what can't be in question is your intent. What can't be in question is your fight. What can't be in question is how hard you're willing to work. That is non-negotiable.' The ability to show up, even for the shit that no one sees, is key to your success.

WATCH
THE EPISODE

JAMES MILNER

THE COMMITMENT PRINCIPLE

'Whatever we do, we do it a hundred per cent. If we were training, we were training a hundred per cent. If we played, we played at a hundred per cent. When we partied, we partied at a hundred per cent.'

James Milner, today a midfielder for Brighton & Hove Albion, was describing to us what it was like to play under Jürgen Klopp at Liverpool, who joined the club in 2015. 'In his first year, we played Watford away at Christmas,' Milner recounts. 'I was injured. We lost at Watford and when we came back, I was thinking, *How are we going to have the Christmas party? What's the atmosphere going to be like?* The manager said, "We've had a crap result today but this is our Christmas party. It's for the staff more than anything. They work so hard all year round, so we're not going to have faces on."' It worked: the party was a hit.

From the very beginning, Klopp had an unyielding commitment to his team, even when things weren't going to plan. Milner says the Champions League semi-final is a perfect example. The team faced Barcelona – Messi and all – and were hammered 3–0 in the first leg. But Klopp didn't lose faith in his team. 'He comes in and says, "No team in the world really has a chance to overturn this. But it's you, and we do."'

'We went to Newcastle on the Saturday, and we scored late to win the game, which kept us in the title [race].' But their rivals Manchester City then won and cemented their spot at the top of the table: 'an absolute balloon buster for us,' Milner deadpanned.

The next day, Klopp was first to training and convened a meeting with his players. 'The manager said, "Does anyone want to say anything about last night?"' The silence in the room was absolute. 'So that was put to bed straight away with one comment,' laughed Milner. 'Done. Then we began the build-up for the match.' Klopp never gave up on his team, so his team never gave up either. 'Straight away, this guy believes in us. There was just a calmness about the game.'

The result was an unprecedented sense of commitment – one that would, with time, take the club to greatness. 'It was never a feeling of desperation,' Milner told us. 'It was just bit by bit, we grew and grew.' And eventually, they grew into Champions League and Premier League winners.

Milner's description of the culture at Liverpool reminded us of the work of two renowned psychologists, Dr John Meyer and Dr Natalie Allen. The pair found three different approaches that can make individuals feel psychologically committed to their team and their organisation as a whole.[1] But not every approach is equal.

THE COMMITMENT PRINCIPLE

The first type is 'continuance commitment', which is driven by a sense of loss. It often occurs when an individual weighs up the pros and cons of leaving a team and reaches the conclusion that the loss you would suffer by leaving – be it friendships, salary or experiences – outweighs the benefits you could obtain by taking on a new role. But this type of commitment often results in higher levels of unhappiness and dissatisfaction with their work.[2]

The second kind of commitment is called 'normative commitment'. This occurs when you mainly feel an overriding sense of obligation to others. The main motivation behind this is a feeling of guilt, feeling that leaving the organisation could harm its performance or put more strain on colleagues. However, research suggests that loyalty alone is not enough to motivate you to do a consistently good job, especially when pursuing long-term ambitions. While these feelings of guilt and obligation can extend an individual's length of service, it can also increase the likelihood of stress and dissatisfaction at work.[3]

The final type of commitment – and the one that seemed to be dominant in Klopp's Liverpool – is called 'affective commitment'. It occurs when you have a deep emotional connection to your team, the values you both uphold and to the nature of the work that you do. In other words, it's when you decide that you genuinely want to be there through the ups and downs. When this alignment happens, the chances of enjoying your work and feeling satisfied in your job increase massively, which, in turn, creates a positive cycle of feeling higher levels of affective commitment.[4] It is the strongest type of commitment of all.

This, it felt to us, was what Klopp had created at Liverpool – and it would prove integral to the success of the club. Meyer and Allen emphasise a handful of simple characteristics that are hallmarks of affective commitment cultures. First, a clear sense of purpose: tick – in his first press conference, the charismatic German famously declared he wanted to turn doubters into believers. Second, strong relationships within the team: tick – 'We went to Dubai as a team and we had a team picture on a boat, which was pinned up in the dressing room,' Milner told us. And third, a consistent pattern of honouring small commitments, even to the things that, at first glance, don't matter: tick – remember 'we party at one hundred per cent'?

So, another clean sweep for Klopp's Liverpool. We weren't sure whether the great manager had ever heard of affective commitment. But one thing is for sure: if his objective was to create a deep sense of commitment to Liverpool FC from its players, the world's leading commitment psychologists couldn't have come up with a better method.[5]

WATCH
THE EPISODE

ALUN WYN JONES

THE IKEA EFFECT

What does the most-capped player in the 150-year history of rugby union have in common with a flat-pack IKEA box?

This is not the first question that came to mind when we sat in front of Alun Wyn Jones, the towering former player who spent ten years as one of the most dominant players in rugby union, playing for the Ospreys, the Wales national team, as well as the British & Irish Lions. But with time, it became the one we found ourselves fixating on.

'I think working hard is a talent,' the mellifluous Welshman was telling us on the podcast. 'If you can work harder than the next person, that is the ultimate talent because it gives you the ability to learn or work on anything.' Ultimately, he says, it was this work ethic that enabled him to succeed. 'I wasn't the most athletically gifted – I knew I had to work at doing that and I was prepared to do that.'

What did this work ethic look like in practice, we

wondered? 'I invested in myself,' Wyn Jones explained. Even as a junior player, he saw his career as something that was down to him alone. 'When I was going away on school trips I'd have my own first-aid kit, just so I didn't need to go to anyone. I became quite self-sufficient early on,' he said. He maintained this emphasis on self-sufficient hard work as he progressed into the paid ranks of his sport. 'When I got to professional level, I was like, "keep reinvesting in yourself," whether it was a piece of gear or whether it was yoga or whatever.'

This conscientious approach wasn't always well received by his teammates. Wyn Jones told us that in training sessions his desire to seek every possible advantage raised some eyebrows. While other players would wearily trudge from one training activity to the next, he would 'sprint from one drill to another. Why not?' he surmised. 'It was extra fitness to me. I wanted to squeeze every last drop. Some people probably didn't like it, but then I think I was trying to earn their respect.'

And yet almost immediately it started to pay off. Within a year of his professional debut, Wyn Jones had started to earn the recognition he sought and was selected to travel to Argentina with the national team. 'I thought I was just going for experience,' he reasoned. 'Maybe sneak on the bench in the second test.' Instead, he watched his coach unveil his name on an old overhead projector showing who would be in the starting line-up. 'I remember it. I got capped at six.' His eyes began to brim with tears as he recounted the significance of this moment. 'When you get that first cap you become one of 1,046 players to play for Wales in 130 years. It's a small number.'

OK, but what does all this have to do with boxes? Well, Alun's hyper-intensive work ethic reminded us of a famous Swedish furniture store and a lesser-known psychological concept named after it: the IKEA effect. This term was coined by researchers Michael I. Norton, Daniel Mochon and Dan Ariely in a 2012 paper named 'The IKEA Effect' in honour of the do-it-yourself furniture company. It described a series of experiments to explore the psychological effect of assembling different products in different contexts.[1]

In one study, the participants were asked to construct three different products: origami, Lego sets and IKEA boxes. Then they were asked to rate how much they liked these products compared to ones they *hadn't* constructed themselves – a paper creation made by a professional origami master, for example.

They discovered something intriguing. Ariely and his peers found that the *amount of work* someone had put into a product had a vast impact on *how highly they rated it*. The participants consistently valued their own self-assembled products more highly than the products that were pre-assembled. This effect occurred even with the construction of plain, boring boxes that didn't have any distinguishing features. In the origami study, the participants even valued their own origami creations as highly as the creations made by certified origami experts. On the flipside, the researchers found that successfully completing tasks was crucial to the

IKEA effect: when people failed to complete the box-building project or destroyed their Lego creations, the effect of falling in love with their own efforts instantly disappeared.

What was the lesson of all this? Well, that hard work is a virtuous circle – the harder we work at something, the more joy we get out of it. And the more joy we get out of something, the harder we are prepared to work at it. It's not just that hard work pays off – it's that when hard work pays off, it leads to even more hard work.

This, it seemed to us, was what was going on with Alun's career. The harder he worked, the more he got out of rugby union – and the more he got out of rugby union, the harder he was prepared to work. He had turned his playing career into a perpetual-motion machine of better and better results. 'To have success early on made me realise that if I do this much more work, what can I get to?' he told us. 'There's a formula that I can create for me to keep going.'

This insight would drive Alun to unprecedented rugby greatness – that day in Argentina marked the first of what would eventually become a breathtaking total of 171 caps, comprising 158 caps for Wales and 13 caps for the British & Irish Lions. And he has never looked back. 'I don't think I ever dreamed I'd play for Wales,' Alun told us. 'My father and grandfather played rugby and we'd have many a Sunday talking about the great stories of the seventies ... To be the only son of a family and play for your country ...' he shook his head. 'You're not representing yourself, you're representing your family, ultimately.'

What's the key insight for anyone who wants to follow suit, we wondered? 'It's about input versus output,' Alun told us. 'Long hours mean something as long as you get something out at the end of the day. Once I realised rugby was my channel to express myself, I thought, *If I work hard enough and keep working, there's opportunities that you can make for yourself.*

WATCH
THE EPISODE

STEVEN GERRARD

ALL IN

James Milner wasn't the only one to build an intense sense of commitment to Liverpool FC. Indeed, Steven Gerrard developed a bond with Liverpool from the age of eight – the first time he represented the city he lived in.

'Very early on, I had a very competitive side,' Gerrard told us on the podcast. 'Liverpool obviously liked that. I'd do anything to come out on top, anything to make sure that I was the winner. I certainly had an obsession to get to Liverpool's first team. I think that got stronger and stronger as I was getting older.'

Once he was there, he maintained a vice-like grip on his place for the next fifteen years, eventually becoming a captain. The captaincy was more than just a job for Gerrard – it was a chance to serve a team he had spent his whole life backing. The people he doesn't want to let down are the ones in the city in which he has grown up. 'Sometimes I would stop on the drive home from Melwood and just sit in the car and tell myself, "I'm captain of Liverpool football club." For a kid who grew up in Huyton, who stood on the Kop, being Liverpool captain is an unbelievable honour,' he wrote in his autobiography. 'I think of all the greats who have led out Liverpool, real leaders like Ron Yeats, Emlyn Hughes, Phil Thompson, Graeme Souness, Alan Hansen. And now me.'[1]

And like these greats, he knew what he was about. When we asked him to sum up his approach to leading teams, he was as succinct and precise as his on-field passing. 'Two words: all in. I want the people to be proud, and to see that I was one of them, and I was all in. I done me best.'

Gerrard's emphasis on absolute all-in commitment to the cause is not limited to Liverpool FC. In fact, it's one of the most evidence-based ways to get results – getting people to make a loud, costly, perhaps public declaration of commitment to a cause. And then keeping on reminding them of it.

This was a method adopted by the famed, serial-winning basketball coach Phil Jackson, who would begin a season by gathering all of the starred members of his team together, drawing a line and then asking each one to step across the line to demonstrate their commitment to following him as their coach. He would begin the symbolic ceremony by stating, 'For that season, I'd ask them to commit to being coached that season by saying, "God has ordained me to coach you young men, and I embrace the role I've been given. If you wish to accept the game I embrace and follow my coaching, as a sign of your commitment, step across that line."

'The essence of coaching is to get the players to wholeheartedly agree to being coached, then offer them a sense of their destiny as a team,' he said.[2] And this approach works. Weight-loss studies have found that when people make a public pledge, like Jackson's basketball players, it helps them to maintain their promise to perform a particular behaviour, such as eating fruit or exercising regularly.[3]

In his book *Influence*, psychologist Robert Cialdini identifies this power of commitment as one of our most important assets when pursuing high performance. Cialdini states, 'Once we have made a choice or taken a stand, we will encounter personal and interpersonal pressures to behave consistently with that commitment. Those pressures will cause us to respond in ways that justify our earlier decision.'[4]

Steven Gerrard would have another turn of phrase for that phenomenon, in even fewer words: *all in*.

WATCH
THE EPISODE

11

How to Rest

MICRO-HABITS

Rest is not a sign of weakness. It is the guarantee of strength.

JOE WICKS

RETIRE EVERY YEAR

'Don't wait till you're older to retire. Have many retirements every year.'

We were immediately taken by Joe Wicks' approach to rest, and not just because he was delivering it with his famous megawatt smile. 'You know, like little moments when things slow down ... Otherwise, you look around and you can achieve so much success – but how much time have you spent with your family and friends?'

'You can achieve so much success – but how much time have you spent with your family and friends?' Joe Wicks

Wicks would know about the perils of one's career getting in the way of your family life. His own dizzying rise to renown accelerated during the Covid-19 pandemic, when his 'PE with Joe' YouTube series, providing daily exercise routines for children and families during lockdowns, became a global sensation. 'It's easy to get caught up in success,' he observed. 'When you start having it, you think, *Is it going to last for ever? I've got to be hot all the time. I need to be popping all the time.*' Eventually, it started to take its toll. 'You can't be like that all the time and not expect something to be sacrificed.'

Wicks offered a simple analogy to emphasise his point. 'Not everything in nature blooms all the time. Everything, whether it's the trees, whether it's plants, they have their moment and then they go and recover and rejuvenate.'

Wicks' observation on the importance of frequent rest is substantiated by rigorous research. The science increasingly shows that rest is not a sign of weakness. It is the guarantee of strength. William Helton, a renowned professor of human factors and applied cognition at George Mason University in Fairfax, Virginia, devised a simple test to show how short breaks can dramatically improve attention.[1] Participants in the test had to stare at railway line maps on a screen for forty-five minutes, which required continuous focus as they tracked the expected train routes.

One group did not receive a break, whereas another was given a five-minute break halfway through the activity, which consisted of a random choice of sitting quietly, listening to music or watching a music video. They were not allowed to leave the room. Regardless of what they did during this break, all of the students who were granted a break fared better on the attention task than those who were forced to continue working without a break.

'Prolonged work seems to be depleting. You start to fade out and there's a decline in performance,' Helton summarises.

'We don't know exactly what in the brain gets depleted, but when you do a cognitively demanding task, it operates as though there's a "mental fuel" that gets burned up.'[2] This process of cognitive depletion has a tremendous impact on our ability to learn. In one study of Danish schoolchildren, when tests took place shortly after the kids had enjoyed a twenty-minute break their scores improved by the equivalent of an extra nineteen days of school.[3]

So what can we all do to draw upon the science of 'mini-retirements' in practice? This term, originally coined by lifestyle strategist Tim Ferriss,[4] challenges the traditional idea that we should work flat out for forty years, then rest. Instead, he suggests we should build in regular periods of time – ranging from a few days to several months, if possible – to step away from work entirely. Not to collapse, but to *reconnect* with ourselves, loved ones and unconnected activities that we enjoy. Ferriss emphasises that these breaks aren't holidays in the conventional sense – they're intentional pauses designed to restore our sense of perspective, recalibrate our goals and return to our work with more energy and not simply more emails.

The good news? You don't have to disappear to start working out how you can go to Bali for three months to get the benefits. A mini-retirement could look like a month off in between projects, a summer sabbatical or simply blocking off every Friday for six weeks to explore something new, such as volunteering, painting or learning a language. What matters most is the *intention*. The willingness to temporarily stop and ask: Is this still the life I want to live?

Wicks' instinct to pause, reflect and realign echoes this

MICRO-HABITS

mindset. By scattering these moments throughout the year – mini-retirements, not mini-breaks, remember – we create a pace that's more sustainable. Like the trees he talked about, we all need seasons. Sometimes it's time to grow, at others it's time to harvest. Occasionally, it's time to rest. As Joe Wicks learned, performance isn't just about how hard you can push, it's also about knowing when to stop so you can start again.

WATCH
THE EPISODE

VICKY PATTISON

NUMBER YOUR DAYS

'Don't count the days, make the days count,' is a powerful exhortation, once delivered by the great boxer Muhammad Ali, seeking to remind us to live with intention and purpose and transform how we experience time.

The big question is, how? Fortunately for us, *Geordie Shore* superstar Vicky Pattison, a woman who has experienced a number of knockdowns and setbacks in her own career, sat down with us to share a simple trick she had discovered on how to do precisely this.

'I used to think that in order to be successful,' Pattison told us, 'I had to be the first one there, I had to know everybody's name, I was going to leave last, I was going to be respectful, polite and,' she paused for breath, 'I was going to do that every single day. There was no place for days off.' In some ways, this routine worked for Vicky. She made her TV debut on *Geordie Shore* at just twenty-three and continued through to her being crowned Queen of the Jungle in the final public vote on the fifteenth series of *I'm a Celebrity . . . Get Me Out of Here!* Pattison has since become a successful podcaster and bestselling author, including penning one book titled *The Secret to Happy*.

But the pace she was living at soon became unsustainable. 'I can't go on like that for ever,' she reasoned. 'It's so counterproductive to have that train of thought. All you do is burn yourself out and lose the love for anything that you were originally passionate about.'

Vicky had to learn not to make every day count, but to number the days. 'Before I explain it,' she modestly began, 'I'm going to hold my hands up and say, I can't take any credit for it.' It was a technique offered to her by a life coach who was helping her make sense of her life in the whirlwind of public scrutiny. 'I have found it invaluable, especially in the last couple of years.'

Put simply, numbering your days means creating a rating system that will determine the level of activity you intend to do that day. To help illustrate her idea, she offered a colourful description of what each numbered day looked like in her world of television, promotion and incessant media demands.

Number four day: 'Getting up in the morning, doing breakfast telly, going straight from there to radio, from radio to a record of something else, from that to a big event. You get home at midnight knackered. Your feet hurt, you're tired, but you know you've had a great day. You've smashed it! It's high-octane. It's stressful. It's big. You're getting a buzz from it. It's amazing but it's hard. That is a number four day.'

Number three day: 'I do a couple of podcasts. You might

have a photo shoot in the afternoon. It is still quite stressful but not non-stop pressure, pressure, pressure. It still takes it out of you.'

Number two day: 'You don't leave the house. You've just got some Zoom calls in the morning and a podcast in the afternoon. You can fit in a nice dog walk.' She smiled contentedly at the thought. 'Bob's your uncle and Fannie's your aunt. It's a good day.'

Number one day: 'These are the days that I absolutely live for,' she laughed. 'You turn your phone off, you have a digital detox, you watch back-to-back boxsets, like *Emily in Paris*. It's a day where you wear a face mask and you play with the dog. You give in to all of the foods that you haven't been eating that week and all of the things you probably haven't been doing and,' she pauses from detailing her list of indulgences, 'you just totally chill and recharge.'

She explained why this simple system has been so effective in her enduring success. 'It is important to have a mixture of these days. When it comes to having a number four day, you're going to be the best bright, shiny, positive, brilliant version of you. You can't do this if you haven't had your number one days.'

Pattison's hard-earned lesson has been rigorously researched and the findings are stark. When it comes to work–life balance, numerous studies show that the greater the balance between different days 'on' and days 'off', the better the physical and mental health of an individual.[1] In one worldwide study, long working hours were linked to over 745,000 deaths in 2016 from stroke and heart disease – a 29 per cent increase since 2000 in deaths linked to overwork.[2] Even the anticipation of taking a break has a positive impact on our health and counters the harmful effects of stress: it seems that in the weeks leading up to a planned holiday, stress has less of an affect on our bodies, pushing up our heart rate measurably less.[3] Other studies show that taking short holidays – in other words, days numbered one and two – have long-lasting effects, including feeling more relaxed and detached from work, and feeling closer to a partner.[4]

Vicky Pattison's simple habit of numbering her days reminds us that high performance isn't about relentless acceleration to the next goal. It's about knowing when to go full throttle and when to ease off the gas. The truth is, we all have number four days. But if we don't make room for the ones and twos, we risk becoming strangers to ourselves. So, what would it look like to number your days? To plan them not just for output but for the outlook they offer. Because, as Vicky explained, the most successful lives aren't the busiest but the most balanced.

WATCH
THE EPISODE

EDDIE HOWE

REFLECT TO RECONNECT

Eddie Howe is a man who has burnished his formidable reputation by seeking out problems and then solving them in style.

After his football playing career was ended prematurely by injury, he took over the centre of excellence at his parent club, AFC Bournemouth, before being appointed team coach at the age of just twenty-nine. His club faced a considerable problem that would scare more experienced coaches. His willingness to meet it head-on would come to define his reputation as one of the game's great coaches.

Bournemouth were bottom of the football pyramid and lumbered with a 17-point deduction due to financial mismanagement. Bailiffs were knocking on the door. Undaunted, Howe dipped into his own pocket to pay the club's bills and doing the laundry himself. Amazingly, over two spells lasting twelve years, he took the club from the bottom of the English Football League to the highest division, the Premier

League, and then defied sporting gravity by keeping them there for five seasons.

When we met with him, he was at the end of a two-year period of two distinct halves. In the first year, he had stepped away from management to analyse his approach. His problem-solving abilities had seemed to desert him, leading to his team being relegated. 'I decided to take twelve months away to reflect and analyse where I had gone wrong and what I was going to do next,' he told us. In the second, he had been appointed head coach of Newcastle United, one of the game's sleeping giants, where he came in and solved an immediate problem – rescuing an ailing team from a hopeless position – before transforming the club into a resilient, ambitious and winning organisation.

We wanted to know about how the first year's reflections had enabled him to do the second part. 'The first thing I did when we got relegated was mourn and grieve about what had happened,' he said, looking out at his team's home stadium, the magnificent St James's Park. 'It was failure in my eyes and it took me a period to come out of that. I needed to reset and see what I wanted to do.'

Science backs up the power of this kind of pause. As psychologists Sabine Sonnentag and Charlotte Fritz discovered through their Detachment-Recovery Model,[1] real recovery doesn't just come from resting the body but from mentally stepping away from work altogether. Their research found that when people take time off and truly detach they return with sharper thinking, greater emotional resilience and a more constructive outlook on problems. It seems that it's not the absence of pressure that makes the difference, it's the chance to reset how we think about it.

Other research reinforces this point. In one study, professionals who took extended sabbaticals from work experienced reduced levels of stress and a significant boost in psychological resources, such as feelings of greater control, which boosted their passion to master their craft – effects that lingered for months after returning.[2] Crucially, these benefits only emerged when individuals used the time to reflect, explore and mentally recharge. In other words, doing exactly what Eddie Howe had done.

This reset proved to be exactly what Howe needed. He decided to engage in a rigorous bout of self-analysis. 'I'd just gone through a really intense period of twelve years in management, where you don't get time to even blink. I wanted to understand what did I do wrong.' How? 'I'm very honest and open with myself, and I asked people that I know to critique me and give me feedback.'

This exploration of his own approach would prove fruitful. 'I needed to improve, and part of that was through education. When you are working you're always reacting, you are always planning, always preparing, but you're not investing in yourself and working on any potential weaknesses that you might have. In my analysis, there were definitely things that I'd neglected.' In particular, he had lost track of what made his approach special. During this period he realised 'my unique selling point,' he said. 'What I think I do best is coach and develop,' he explained. 'I love helping people. I love developing footballers and trying to help change their lives.'

This was the approach he soon brought to Newcastle. 'The culture of any organisation determines its success,' he said in one interview. 'It's all about how people interact with each other, and you can stimulate that with little things to get them talking and mixing in different groups. Everything we do is about making a better working environment and stimulating respect.'[3]

As such, he instigated some simple but powerful methods to create a culture of 'love and care' at Newcastle. Each time his team wins three points, Howe routinely asks all non-playing substitutes and squad members to join off-field staff and injured players in posing for a group photograph alongside those who actually played. This picture will be displayed in the team's training base. 'It's part of the culture we're trying to create: a culture in which everyone's in it together. It's not just about the first eleven on the pitch – everyone at the club plays a huge part in any success.'[4]

'It's not just about the first eleven on the pitch – everyone at the club plays a huge part in any success.' Eddie Howe

The effects of small changes like these were immediate. Soon after he came to Newcastle United, newly acquired and minted with Saudi Arabian investment, the play of many players, such as the Brazilian Joelinton and Spaniard Miguel Almirón, started to transform. And players who joined the team like Kieran Trippier – an established international and La Liga champion – were soon playing the best football of their careers. As a result, Newcastle went from languishing near the bottom of the league tables to finishing fifth two years later – and winning Newcastle their first major UK trophy in seven decades, the EFL Cup.

By taking some time to reset and reflect on losses and wins alike, Howe was able to transform his own performance – and that of one of England's greatest football clubs.

WATCH
THE EPISODE

EMILY MAITLIS

GOLDEN TIME

Emily Maitlis concedes that she will forever be linked to one famous interview. In 2019, the BBC gave her the responsibility of interviewing Prince Andrew, the Queen's second son, who was embroiled in a scandal that threatened to engulf him and the Royal Family. At Andrew's behest, Maitlis was despatched to Buckingham Palace to interview him and to establish the facts about his links to the late child sex offender Jeffrey Epstein.

The interview went well for Maitlis and badly for Andrew – who memorably claimed that he couldn't have spent one crucial evening with an alleged victim because he was at a Pizza Express in Woking. Andrew was sent into a disgraced exile while Maitlis was heralded for her fearless ability to ask the difficult questions.

How, we asked, did she learn to perform under such acute pressure? 'I hid in the loo,' she told us. 'I hid in the loo!'

'I'm not really joking,' she went on after we raised our eyebrows. 'A good interview is made in the five-minute silence that you spend on your own before it. It's golden time.'

She explained why this time was so important. 'As soon as you arrive, you're shown into a room. In this case, a Buckingham Palace ballroom.' She described the blizzard of frenetic activity that followed. 'Everything starts: there's people checking make-up, there's lights, there's somebody mic'ing you up, there's people coming to shake hands.

'It's all helpful, but you lose your silence, right?' And so she needed to get out. 'I suddenly realised that I just wasn't ready. I wanted five minutes on my own. So I excused myself and I asked "Is there a ladies?"'

Once there, she embraced the solitude. 'I locked the door and I remember just sitting in the corner going, "Where's my head? How do I find clarity? How do I just let everything go silent?"'

'How do I find clarity? How do I just let everything go silent?' Emily Maitlis

Maitlis explained to us how this moment of silence had a transformative impact. 'I had thirty questions, but then you think, *What's the purpose?* We always say that in news if you can't tell a story in five words, it's probably not the right story.' And it was in these five minutes that it all came together.

Pizza Express in Woking. The inability to sweat. The friendship with a convicted paedophile. The story emerged through Maitlis's five minutes of golden time.

Maitlis is not the only one to have noticed the power of these quiet moments. Recent research has demonstrated that when we intentionally seek out and embrace moments of silence, it helps heal our nervous system, build our energy levels and allow our thinking to be more flexible and open to difficult personal and professional situations. Indeed, Imke Kirste of Duke University School of Medicine recently discovered that silence promotes the growth of new cells in the hippocampus, the brain region related with learning and memory.[1]

A few moments of quiet 'golden time' can even diffuse the most fraught arguments. In one series of experiments, researchers prompted couples to argue and then, when they were in the midst of their disagreement, the scientists informed them that the experiment had to be stopped in order to fix the recording equipment. The warring pair were taken to a waiting area and encouraged to read or listen to music before returning to the room a few minutes later. When they did, they entered as emotionally different people.[2] It seems that the short break helped the raw emotions to settle, causing the resulting discussion to be more compassionate and understanding.

Emily Maitlis's experience underscores the significance of creating a space for reflection when under pressure. In moments of silence, she said, 'sometimes you just have this blinding clarity. I can't explain it any other way.' She is not the only one. We can all benefit from the power of golden time.

WATCH
THE EPISODE

12

How to Stay Optimistic

MICRO-HABITS

If you can stay positive during the dark times, success will find you in the light.

JAMES TIMPSON

CELEBRATE THE GOOD NEWS FIRST

James Timpson is the CEO of the eponymous Timpson Group, a UK-based retail services company known for shoe repairs, key cutting and other high street services. Under his leadership – which he dubs 'upside-down management' – the company has embraced a distinctive culture centred on employee welfare and social responsibility. He advocates for a decentralised management style with only two rules:

1. Look the part
2. Put the money in the till

Apart from that, he allows them to get on with it. Timpson's approach has not only driven business growth but also garnered recognition for the company's progressive and humane employment policies. He has offered a beacon of light on the British high street through numerous downturns – and made his brand famous for its positive community impact. Over the years, Timpson have offered to dry clean – for free – the suits of the unemployed going for job interviews, employed countless people leaving prison and generally lived up to the company's tagline: Great Service by Great People.

When we sat down with James at his home in the Cheshire countryside, we were interested in what he thought drove his company forwards. His answer: focus on the good news.

His father, John, had created a newsletter for his business in 1987. 'It was just a letter of bad news,' James told us. 'He would get pretty down because it was just more bad news after the other.' Eventually, he decided to try something new. 'He did these little notepads saying: Send some good news. He sent it to every shop . . . and it all started coming in: "I've had a record week" or "my daughter's passed a driving test" or "I'm getting married".

'That formed the basis of the newsletter, which is just good news,' James told us. The newsletter is still going today.

James's eyes blazed as he spoke about the effects of this simple initiative. 'I sometimes get challenged on the fact that it's a bit cult-like. Have we just done too much good news? For example, I have opened shops that have been a complete disaster. I have bought businesses that have been a complete disaster. I feel I probably make more mistakes than most people do, but it's about being positive and being on the front foot and being honest about when things go wrong.'

The idea of blowing your own trumpet may feel a little arrogant – even a little American, perhaps. But there is scientific proof that sharing good news stories has numerous positive psychological effects. 'Discussing positive experiences leads to heightened well-being, increased overall life satisfaction, and even more energy,' one study in the *Journal of Social and Personal Relationships* reports.[1]

So, what can you do to share good news a little more widely in your own world? The answer might be to create a simple ritual – whether it's a weekly team meeting, a family dinner or even a WhatsApp group with friends – and build in a moment where people are invited to share one thing that's gone well. What matters is not the scale of the win but the habit of celebrating it. And as James Timpson shows, the ripple effects can be remarkable. It not only lifts performance – it also raises the spirit of a team.

WATCH
THE EPISODE

SARINA WIEGMAN

ATTITUDE: GRATITUDE

When Sarina Wiegman led the Lionesses to victory in the 2021 European Championships, she ended fifty-five years of hurt. The roar that rang out across Wembley Stadium was echoed around the country as millions of fans cheered at the team's victory over Germany. And the support she received was no less uproarious when she repeated the accomplishment four years later.

For Wiegman, this support was everything. One of the team's longest-serving players was Jill Scott, who told us how Wiegman had observed a simple win. 'She stopped us after one of our friendly games and said, "I didn't really see people clapping the crowd before the game. We need to do that more and get them behind us."'

This was different advice from most coaches. 'We'd always been told, "Don't play to the occasion,"' Scott explained. '"Really focus when we get out there for the warm-up; don't acknowledge the crowd until the end of the game."' Wiegman was different. 'Her spin was about getting

ATTITUDE: GRATITUDE

them behind us,' Scott said. And the effect on the players was instant. 'It just worked. The crowds loved it and then we got more support the next game.'

When we got Wiegman on the podcast, we asked her to explain this thinking. 'When I was an international player, we were happy when there were 5,000 people coming to watch us,' she said. 'Now, the game has changed so much, with lots of people coming out. I thought, *we should be really grateful and happy*, which we were.'

It wasn't that she didn't understand the players' concerns, she told us: 'They thought that I would think they weren't focused on football when they would wave to the fans.' But that wasn't really the point of her request. 'I said, "You better go out and wave because they took the effort to come and support us. I know you're such professionals that when you go out there you wave and then you start your warm-up – I'm not thinking you're not focused on football."'

Her goal, ultimately, was to change their focus – away from the overwhelming pressure of the game and towards their gratitude to simply be playing. 'They felt a little uncomfortable, I think. The players were not used to that. They had learned that we first have to perform, and then we can wave. I said, "Just turn it around. You can also do it if you do well after the game."'

There is some compelling science behind Wiegman's approach. We have known for years that the psychological benefits of expressing gratitude and appreciation are significant, especially when it comes to dealing with stress and developing a resilience to persevere in the face of challenges: qualities which the Lionesses showed in abundance. And it's not just about your mood: the research increasingly indicates that if you can stay positive during the dark times, success will find you in the light.

In one study, a group of people older than sixty were separated into three groups. The first group was directed to write messages of gratitude to others, the second to write down their worries, and the third to do a 'neutral' assignment, writing about something else entirely. Following that, each group was subjected to reminders of their death and other messages intended to induce anxiety about their mortality. The first group, who had deliberately practised their gratitude were 'immunised' from death anxiety much more than the other two groups.[1]

So perhaps Sarina Wiegman was on to something. Sometimes, we all need a little reminder of how powerful and vital expressing gratitude is. After all, it worked for the Lionesses. 'You play at the highest level and it's an absolute privilege that you're allowed to play for 80,000 people,' Sarina said. 'We had better enjoy it.'

WATCH
THE EPISODE

SARA PASCOE

UNCONDITIONAL POSITIVE REGARD

Most stand-up comedy audiences are like grizzly bears: they are definitely ravenous, and either looking to be fed with entertaining morsels or, alternatively, to eat you alive. Until you see them, it tends not to be clear which.

That is why, for at least one of your authors, performing a stand-up set sounds like a horrible nightmare. But somehow, Sara Pascoe's whimsical comedy has successfully managed to keep her audiences sated for fourteen years, without undermining the stellar writing and acting career she has created on the side. When we sat with her, she was about to embark on an epic UK tour, yet seemed completely unphased by the 47-date bear pit she was about to step into.

We asked her how she managed to remain so calm despite the pressure of making tens of thousands of people laugh every night. 'I think that's where self-esteem comes in,' she claimed. 'If I go out and have a bad show somewhere, I now don't go home saying "I'm a bad comedian." I go, "I'm a person who now has a toolbox and I still didn't have what I needed tonight."'

Gaining such healthy perspective has come slowly. It has been obtained by developing a willingness to face what comedians dramatically call 'dying on stage'. 'I remember my first gig to silence,' she said, grimacing at the memory. 'I followed a dog jumping up at a balloon. The mistake I made was thinking: *If they like this dog jumping up at a balloon, imagine how much they're going to like me with my words.*

'What I should have done is comment on the fact I was following a dog jumping up at a balloon. He absolutely smashed it. Instead, what happened is I just went into my material, which I was confident of. They just stared at me and I'd never had a gig to absolute silence before.' She paused to emphasise her point. 'This is absolute failure.'

This bruising experience burned deep in her memory. 'It feels horrific and you've got nothing else to do,' she said. 'What I should have done was stopped doing material and commented on the fact it wasn't working. But at that point, I would have been far too scared to do that. Five minutes in that scenario is very, very long.'

She described how it feels to stand in front of a very-much-not-laughing audience in these moments. 'Hearing your own voice really loud in your head while you're also talking. Have you ever had that?' she asked. We both nodded in uncomfortable recognition. 'This is low performance.'

So how did Sara convince herself to go back out on stage? Well, one of the techniques Pascoe adopted is one first identified in the 1940s by Carl Rogers, a humanistic psychologist, to support therapists when treating distressed patients in counselling. It is known as 'unconditional positive regard'.[1]

Rogers believed that dysfunctional behaviours, such as overeating, excessive drinking and procrastination, aren't altered with harsh confrontation, strident judgements or robust punishments. Being bullied, shamed or judged for our behavioural flaws merely stunts our growth. Instead, they are far better dealt with through exposure to more positive emotions: the likes of compassion, understanding and acceptance.

'Unconditional positive regard' refers to how a therapist should approach listening to a patient. It requires them to adopt a complete and non-judgemental acceptance, regardless of what the other person may say or do. Rogers suggests that this open-minded approach helps plant a seed of hope. Only then, when we begin to feel safe, can honesty follow. According to Rogers, this is the crucial first step to change our behaviour.

This method is not about pretending to like a client or unquestioningly accepting everything they have done. But it does require a therapist to begin by respecting the client as a human being with their own free will. It also demands that the therapist assumes that their patient is doing the best they can in that moment.

It seemed to us that Pascoe had taken this method and simply applied it to herself. In fact, unconditional positive regard is as good as any way of describing her belief in her own talents. 'I have to tell myself really wonderful things like, "I'm so lucky to do this job. I wanted to be here. No one's making me be here. I could have pulled out of this gig. I don't need the money. I'm here because I love it,"' she explained.

She also emphasised the importance of keeping a positive approach to her audience. 'I remind myself that I love human beings. I tell you who I really love: human beings who leave the house to go and watch stuff.' And she then liberally showers them with unconditional positive thoughts. 'Why do we leave the house? It's so nice at home. The weather's terrible. There's amazing stuff on TV. These people got childcare or made an arrangement or even came by themselves. Why are you scared of them? You're in love with these people.'

> 'Why are you scared of them? You're in love with these people.' Sara Pascoe

Researchers have found that this kind of unconditional positive regard has countless benefits. The behaviour expert Nir Eyal cites one study of young athletes which found that those who received unconditional positive regard from their coaches were more motivated to continue playing sports without prompting and reported feeling more confident when they did take to the field. When faced with setbacks, they consistently responded positively and then looked to take on new challenges.[2] On the other hand, those athletes who were subjected to regular criticism were found to feel less secure, less motivated and more likely to burn out. This mirrors a similar trend found in education, where students who received unconditional positive regard from their teachers were more motivated to persevere at tasks until they eventually enjoyed success.[3]

UNCONDITIONAL POSITIVE REGARD

What's the alternative to unconditional positive regard? We may fall subject to bleak, worst-case scenarios that do not serve us. 'I used to have this horrible thing where I used to imagine that half of my audience had been dragged there by someone,' said Pascoe. 'Men, dragged by their wives, who don't think women are funny. That is so useless to my brain!'

But there is another way. 'Believing they've come in a positive frame of mind means you have to meet them in a positive frame of mind too,' Pascoe argued. Choosing to believe the best is what enables you to truly *be* your best.

**WATCH
THE EPISODE**

JASON FOX

WHAT WOULD A COMMANDO DO?

Jason Fox describes himself as a normal bloke who has learned to thrive in abnormal circumstances. He served for over twenty years in the British army, first as a marine and later in the special forces. Since leaving, he has battled the effects of PTSD to forge a career within the media as a presenter and celebrated author.

This is not the life that Fox anticipated having, he told us on the podcast. 'I grew up as a normal kid,' he explained. 'An extremely uninspiring person. I learned an awful lot – and I experienced an awful lot – in the military.'

It was these experiences in the military that eventually helped Fox feel 'superhuman'. 'What we all have in common is we're all human, regardless of how we come into this world and what we go on to do. The superhuman bit was just me understanding that I could control how I operated and respond to things.'

WHAT WOULD A COMMANDO DO?

He maintains that this state of feeling superhuman is possible for everyone to achieve. 'I think that anyone can get to a certain point where they feel that they're superhuman in relation to whatever it is that they're dealing with.'

In Fox's own case, developing his own superpowers involved learning to think like a commando. 'When you join up as a young recruit, you think it's all about how to strip your weapon down in ten seconds and put it back together blindfolded. Yet, the first thing that they pretty much teach you is to embrace a culture to live by.'

What did this culture look like, we asked? 'In the marines there's something that they call the "commando spirit",' he said. 'It's made up of four parts: courage, determination, unselfishness and cheerfulness in the face of adversity.'

These qualities – especially the courage and determination elements – were first put to the test when he joined as a callow sixteen-year-old and immediately had to confront his fear of heights. 'The marines do an awful lot of their work at height,' he explained. 'You climb cliffs, you abseil, jump out of helicopters. I needed to deal with that pretty quickly.' The commando spirit is what allowed him to survive.

Of course, telling people to take on a 'commando spirit' is simple – getting them to actually live up to it is harder, especially when you are 1,000 feet in the air. But that was where the marines used a surprising and intriguing method. He told us that whenever he was facing adversity, the captains would ask a simple question: What would a commando do? This, Fox explained 'is drummed into you'.

He shared the example of how he demonstrated these

traits during his arduous record-breaking row across the Atlantic Ocean, which he completed with three mates, including his fellow marine – and *High Performance* guest – Aldo Kane.

Each man would row for two hours and rest for two hours on a 24-hour cycle, lasting weeks. Despite capsizing three times, fighting hypothermia and battling severe sleep deprivation, Fox asked himself that all-important question. He exemplified the commando unselfishness by ending his rest period early. He would get Kane's bed ready, put toothpaste on his brush and make life as easy as possible for his exhausted teammate to get his own much-needed sleep. The key, he maintains, was to do this series of small but significant selfless acts without expectation of it being reciprocated. 'I don't like the word "react",' he explained when reflecting on these moments. 'Reacting is not great. I *responded* to the things that I was trained to do.' In short: he responded as a commando would do.

'I don't like the word "react". Reaction is not great. I *responded*.' Jason Fox

This may sound simple, but it worked for Fox – and science can explain why. There is a growing body of work indicating that when you take yourself out of your own mindset – *What would someone like* me *do?* – and into the mindset of another person – *What would a* commando *do?* – you can transform your ability to handle difficult situations.

WHAT WOULD A COMMANDO DO?

In one study described in the journal *Psychology Today*,[1] researchers assigned groups of four- to six-year-old children a series of boring tasks and told them to focus on them for as long as they could. The researchers also told them that they could take a break whenever they wanted – and even provided a game on a tablet for them to play instead.

The children were then divided into three groups. The first were told to regularly ask themselves, 'Am I working hard?' The second were told to refer to themselves in the third person and ask themselves, 'Is [their own name] working hard?' Finally, group three were given a choice of a topical character they associated with hard work, such as Batman, Bob the Builder or Dora the Explorer. They were asked to regularly question whether their *character* was working hard.

Perhaps unsurprising, the children who referred to themselves in the first person were the least productive. The children who referred to themselves in the third person did a little better. But the children in the third group performed better than everyone: by taking on the *character* of a high performer they also managed to take on the *characteristics* of that high performer. As *Psychology Today* summarised it: 'Taking on the characteristics of a hardworking character gave them confidence that they could keep going.'[2]

Why does this approach work? It's a little unclear. But Ethan Kross, professor of psychology at the University of Michigan, suggests that even taking small shifts in perspective can help people to separate themselves from their emotions and establish a greater sense of control. It's not you struggling with the challenge before you – it's a commando. And a commando would probably handle it very differently.

WATCH
THE EPISODE

EPILOGUE

The Twelve-Month Micro-Habits Plan

MICRO-HABITS

The road to success starts with the smallest steps.

I love you.
It's a girl.
He's dead.

The most dramatic, emotionally charged moments of your life didn't begin with lengthy speeches. More often, they began with short, succinct, simple sentences.

In the same way, the most powerful changes don't start with grand declarations of intent, but instead they begin with something much smaller: a shift in focus; a change in your perspective or a single, quiet question that makes you think.

This has not been a book encouraging you to transform everything about your life. Rather, we asked you to consider starting much smaller. Indeed, everything we've learned over the last few years points to one simple message: that the road to success starts with the smallest steps. That is why the most effective micro-habits contain the three Ss:

Small enough to start now.
Simple enough to do without overthinking it.
Speedy enough to fit into your real life.

So, here's your final step: read these twelve short prompts. Each one is distilled from the specific chapter of the book that's highlighted, and draws on the wisdom of high performers that has been validated by robust scientific study. Each question is designed to act like a catalyst – they are small in size but powerful in impact – to help you decide where to start.

You don't need to do all of them, but decide which one resonates most for where you are *right now* and then sit with it, try it out and, finally, let it lead you towards your own definition of high performance.

1. **What really gets me moving, and how can I use it more often?**
   Read: *How to Motivate Yourself*
2. **What matters most to me, and how clearly does my life reflect that?**
   Read: *How to Find Your Purpose*
3. **Am I busy or am I focused?**
   Read: *How to Focus on What Matters*
4. **Is my time organised around what's urgent or what's important?**
   Read: *How to Organise Your Time (and Your Life)*

5. Who brings out the best in me, and when did I last make time for them?
   Read: *How to Connect with Others*
6. Do I know what makes other people tick, or do I just assume?
   Read: *How to Get the Best Out of People*
7. What's one small habit that could bring my team closer together?
   Read: *How to Build a Close-Knit Team*
8. Do I treat feedback as a tool or a threat?
   Read: *How to Give (and Receive) Better Feedback*
9. What do I do to prepare *before* pressure builds rather than during it?
   Read: *How to Perform Under Pressure*
10. What's one habit that helps me show up even when I don't feel like it?
    Read: *How to Do the Work*
11. Have I truly rested or have I just distracted myself?
    Read: *How to Rest*
12. What's one habit I can practise – even on the hardest days – that gives me hope?
    Read: *How to Stay Optimistic*

High performance isn't about a single moment. It's not what you do occasionally that will define you.

It is about creating a method. It's what you keep doing, especially when no one's watching. It's the shit that people don't see.

MICRO-HABITS

As many of our guests on *High Performance* have demonstrated, the micro-habits they adopted in their past are the stories they share in their future. The same goes for you. Don't wait for the perfect time to begin. Choose your area to focus on, begin building the habit that addresses it and start out along your own unique path to excellence.

ACKNOWLEDGEMENTS

Damian

No book is ever written by one person alone. This one certainly hasn't been.

First, to my family: thank you for your endless patience, humour and love. Geraldine, whose encouragement has been the quiet strength behind every chapter. To George and Rose, who remind me daily of what really matters, and whose questions, laughter and curiosity fuel my own. To Rosemarie, Anthony, Chris, Rachael and Colin and the whole of my family for your interest, support and encouragement. To Teddy for your faithful company and to Auntie Pat and Brian, my dad, for watching over me.

To Jake Humphrey, my co-adventurer in the High Performance journey. Thank you for the friendship, honesty and the countless conversations that have sharpened my thinking.

To Will Murphy-O'Connor, our tireless producer on *High Performance*. Thank you for creating the environment of care, curiosity and collaboration that enables these conversations.

To Louise Jamieson for your support, patience and encouragement. I am immensely grateful.

To the many guests who have shared their stories with

ACKNOWLEDGEMENTS

us – on the podcast, in interviews and in private moments – thank you for your candour, your courage and for trusting me with your truths. This book rests on your shoulders.

To my colleagues and collaborators in sport, business and academia, who have challenged me, supported me and invited me into your worlds. You have helped me see how ideas live in the real world, not just on the page.

To the researchers, psychologists and storytellers whose work I draw upon: you light the path. It has been a privilege to stand on your foundations and bring your insights to a wider audience.

To David Luxton, my endlessly patient literary agent: thank you for your support.

And finally, to the reader – you. Thank you for giving your time, your attention and your open mind. My hope is that what you've read will not just inform, but also inspire, and perhaps even accompany you on your own journey to your own definition of high performance.

Jake

Nobody deserves a mention among these pages more than my wife Harriet. She'll also hate me mentioning that we met in a nightclub in Norwich in 1999! From that moment when our eyes met over an Archers and lemonade (her drink of choice!) you have been a daily source of joy and inspiration for me. The most loyal and loving person I've ever met. A person who gave up on her dreams so me and our children could live theirs – something I will never forget. I love you to infinity and beyond.

To Flo and Seb who have inspired every conversation

ACKNOWLEDGEMENTS

on *High Performance*. 'Does this show leave the world in a better place for our children' is a question Damian and I try and ask about every guest we welcome to the show. You are the real reason for *High Performance* and watching you both grow into incredible young people is the privilege of my life!

Thank you, Damian. The greatest co-host a man could wish for – loving sharing the journey with you.

Mum and Dad – thanks for the roots that keep my compass in the right direction, and the wings that mean I can't stop exploring the world, love you both so much.

Tom, Rachel, Nathan, Dulcie, Abi, John and all my nieces and nephews – the days with you and family are the ones I'll always cherish the most and forever wish I'd had more of.

Hannah – the greatest colleague I could ask for. The energy you have brought to my life and the wider *High Performance* team is incredible. You're a true light in the room and none of this happens without you.

Sunil and David, my Whisper Group co-founders, that journey and business is something I remain so incredibly proud of and one day when we tell the story I know it will inspire so many others.

To my fellow podcasters who have set the bar so high. I'm in awe of you all and you do such amazing work.

Steve – miss you buddy and I think you would have enjoyed this one.

Damian and Jake

We would both like to thank the whole *High Performance* team. Your endless enthusiasm, your indefatigable spirit and

ACKNOWLEDGEMENTS

boundless energy and unfailing humour make a great team and an even greater impact.

We are also hugely grateful to the wider team at YMU – especially Elise Middleton and Briony Gowlett.

Thank you to all our podcast guests, for investing your trust in us and sharing your incredible wisdom, insights and lessons.

Thank you also to our fantastically talented, unfailingly polite and incredibly patient editor, Rowan Borchers. Your advice, direction and guidance has been a privilege to receive. Equally, your faith, trust and support for the *High Performance* message is greatly appreciated. You have shaped rough drafts into something we are proud to share. We also extend our appreciation to the whole team at Penguin Random House for your passionate support of this book.

Finally, we would like to extend our sincere thanks to you, the reader. We never lose sight of the fact that you have a dizzying amount of choice, distraction and demands upon your time and focus. Reading this far in the book demands both. We don't take this lightly. We hope *Micro-Habits* has been as rewarding to read as it has been to write.

NOTES

Introduction: Small, Simple, Speedy

1 This account of Ian McGeechan's career draws upon his autobiography, *Lion Man* (Simon & Schuster, 2010) and Tom English, *The Grudge: Two Nations, One Match, No Holds Barred* (Random House, 2011).

2 E. Stamatakis, M. Ahmadi, R. K. Biswas, et al., 'Device-Measured Vigorous Intermittent Lifestyle Physical Activity (VILPA) and Major Adverse Cardiovascular Events: Evidence of Sex Differences', *British Journal of Sports Medicine*. Published online 28 October 2024. doi.org/10.1136/bjsports-2024-108484.

3 Maksudul Shadat Akash and Shahanaz Chowdhury, 'Small Changes, Big Impact: A Mini Review of Habit Formation and Behavioral Change Principles', *World Journal of Advanced Research and Reviews*, 26 (2025), 3098–3106. doi.org/10.30574/wjarr.2025.26.1.1333.

4 Phillippa Lally, et al., 'How Are Habits Formed: Modelling Habit Formation in the Real World', *European Journal of Social Psychology*, 40.6 (2010), 998–1009.

Phillippa Lally, Jane Wardle and Benjamin Gardner, 'Experiences of Habit Formation: a Qualitative Study', *Psychology, Health & Medicine*, 16.4 (2011), 484–89.

NOTES

5   Alan Bennett, 'I Know What I Like, but I'm Not Sure about Art', *The Independent*, 24 May 1995.

Lando Norris: Job, Career or Calling?

1   Amy Wrzesniewski, Clark McCauley, Paul Rozin, Barry Schwartz, 'Jobs, Careers, and Callings: People's Relations to Their Work', *Journal of Research in Personality*, 31.1 (1997), 21–33.

    Melody Wilding, 'Do You Have a Job, Career or Calling? The Difference Matters', Forbes.com. Published online 23 April 2018.

2   Jane E. Dutton and Amy Wrzesniewski, 'What Job Crafting Looks Like', *Harvard Business Review*. Published online 12 March 2020.

Adam Peaty: The Odysseus Contract

1   This is also referred to as a 'Ulysses Contract' – it is the same thing: Bruce Grierson, 'Writing Your Own "Ulysses Contract"', *Psychology Today*. Published online 2 September 2017.

2   Reported in the *New York Times*, 5 January 2012: 'New Year's Resolutions Stick When Willpower Is Reinforced.'

    'Commitment Contracts: Another Good Way of Helping Us Reach Our Goals', *Good Medicine*.

    C. I. Brimhall, D. Tannenbaum, E. M. VanEpps, 'Choosing More Aggressive Commitment Contracts for Others than for the Self', *Judgment and Decision Making*, 18 (2023), e12. doi.org/10.1017/jdm.2023.1.

    'Put a Bet on It: Self-funded Commitment Contracts Get

People to the Gym,' Lund University School of Economics and Management (LUSEM).

Keely Hodgkinson: Motivation Hacking

1   R. Ryan and E. Deci, 'Self Determination Theory and the Facilitation of Intrinsic Motivation, Social Development, and Well-Being', *American Psychologist*, 55.1 (January 2000), 68–78.
2   Ibid.

Matthew McConaughey: Delayed Gratification

1   W. Mischel, E. B. Ebbesen and A. Raskoff Zeiss, 'Cognitive and Attentional Mechanisms in Delay of Gratification', *Journal of Personality and Social Psychology*, 21.2 (1972), 204–18. doi.org/10.1037/h0032198.
    W. Mischel, *The Marshmallow Test: Mastering Self-Control* (Little, Brown and Co., 2014). psycnet.apa.org/record/2014-43233-000
2   W. Mischel, Y. Shoda and P. K. Peake, 'The Nature of Adolescent Competencies Predicted by Preschool Delay of Gratification', *Journal of Personality and Social Psychology*, 54.4 (1988), 687–96. doi.org/10.1037/0022-3514.54.4.687.
3   Tanya R. Schlam, et al., 'Preschoolers' Delay of Gratification Predicts Their Body Mass 30 Years Later', *The Journal of Pediatrics*, 162.1 (2013), 90–93.
4   Walter Mischel, 'Self-Control Theory', *Handbook of Theories of Social Psychology*, 2 (2012), 1–22.
5   K. Yanaoka, L. E. Michaelson, R. M. Guild, G. Dostart, J. Yonehiro, S. Saito and Y. Munakata, 'Cultures Crossing:

The Power of Habit in Delaying Gratification', *Psychological Science*, 33.7 (2022), 1172–81. doi.org/10.1177/09567976221074650.

6   Ilene Strauss Cohen, 'The Benefits of Delaying Gratification', *Psychology Today*. Published online 26 December 2017. Karoline Lempert, 'Delayed Gratification: Is It About Self-Control or Culture?', *Psychology Today*. Published online 9 August 2023.

Johann Hari: The Cambodian Cow

1   Patrick L. Hill and Nicholas A. Turiano, 'Purpose in Life as a Predictor of Mortality Across Adulthood', *Psychological Science*, 25.7 (2014), 1482–86.

Ed Diener and Micaela Y. Chan, 'Happy People Live Longer: Subjective Well-Being Contributes to Health and Longevity', *Applied Psychology: Health and Well-Being* (2010).

P. L. Hill, N. A. Turiano, D. K. Mroczek, A. L. Burrow, 'The Value of a Purposeful Life: Sense of Purpose Predicts Greater Income and Net Worth', *Journal of Research in Personality*, 65 (2016), 38–42. doi.org/10.1016/j.jrp.2016.07.003.

Dame Stephanie Shirley: The Bedtime Question Worth Asking

1   V. E. Frankl, *Man's Search for Meaning* (Simon & Schuster, 1997).

Ali Abdaal: Write Your Own Obituary

1   Kenneth E. Vail, Jacob Juhl, et al., 'When Death is Good for Life: Considering the Positive Trajectories of Terror

Management', *Personality and Social Psychology Review*, 16.4 (2012), 303–29.

N. J. Kelley, B. J. Schmeichel, 'Thinking about Death Reduces Delay Discounting', *PLOS One*, 10.12 (2015). doi.org/10.1371/journal.pone.0144228. PMID: 26630664; PMCID: PMC4668029.

2 'The Bright Side of Death: Awareness of Mortality Can Result in Positive Behaviors', ScienceDaily.com. Published online 30 April 2012.

Simon Sinek: The Best-Friend Test

1 C. Pezirkianidis, et al., *Frontiers in Psychology*, 14 (2023); R. Blieszner, et al., *Innovation in Aging*, 3.1 (2019); K. W. Choi, et al., *The American Journal of Psychiatry*, 177.10 (2020).

2 J. Holt-Lunstad, et al., *PLOS Medicine*, 7.7 (2010); A. Steptoe, et al., *PNAS*, 110.15 (2013); *Perspectives on Psychological Science*, 10.2 (2015).

Will Guidara: Sweating the Small Stuff

1 For lots of these stories, read Will Guidara's book: *Unreasonable Hospitality: The Remarkable Power of Giving People More Than They Expect,* (Optimism Press, 2022).

2 A. Parasuraman, V. A. Zeithaml and L. L. Berry, 'SERVQUAL: A Multiple-Item Scale for Measuring Consumer Perceptions Of Service Quality', *Journal of Retailing*, 64.1 (1988), 12–40.

R. Ladhari, 'Service Quality, Emotional Satisfaction, and Behavioural Intentions: A Study in the Hotel Industry', *Managing Service Quality*, 19.3 (2009), 308–331.

NOTES

M. J. Bitner, 'Evaluating Service Encounters: The Effects of Physical Surroundings and Employee Responses', *Journal of Marketing*, 54.2 (1990), 69–82.

S. S. Andaleeb, 'Service Quality Perceptions and Patient Satisfaction: A Study Of Hospitals in a Developing Country', *Social Science & Medicine*, 52.9 (2001), 1359–70.

Stuart Broad: Are You Playing to Win?

1 This draws on the research of Edward Tory Higgins. His paper is here: E. Tory Higgins, 'Regulatory Focus Theory', *Handbook of Theories of Social Psychology*, 1 (2012), 483–504. Heidi Grant Halvorson uses this work, which is detailed in her book, *Succeed: How We Can Reach Our Goals* (Hudson, 2010). They also co-authored a book: *Focus: Use Different Ways of Seeing the World for Success and Influence* (Hudson, 2013).

  I also found more info here: 'Do You Play to Win – or to Not Lose?', *Harvard Business Review*. Published March 2013.

2 Henning Plessner, Christian Unkelbach, Daniel Memmert, Anna Baltes, Andreas Kolb, 'Regulatory Fit as a Determinant of Sport Performance: How to Succeed in a Soccer Penalty-Shooting', *Psychology of Sport and Exercise*, 10.1 (2009), 108–115.

3 The quote is from: H. G. Halvorson, E. T. Higgins, 'Do You Play to Win – or to Not Lose?', *Harvard Business Review*, 91.3 (2013), 117–20, 135. PMID: 23451530. One fascinating study on this topic is: Philipp Wolfgang Lichtenthaler and Andrea Fischbach, 'A Meta-Analysis on Promotion- and Prevention-Focused Job Crafting', *European Journal of Work and Organizational Psychology*, 28 (2019), 30–50.

NOTES

4   Henning Plessner, Christian Unkelbach, Daniel Memmert, Anna Baltes, Andreas Kolb, 'Regulatory Fit as a Determinant of Sport Performance: How to Succeed in a Soccer Penalty-Shooting', *Psychology of Sport and Exercise*, 10.1 (2009), 108–115. I also read about this in: H. G. Halvorson, E. T. Higgins, 'Do You Play to Win – or to Not Lose?', *Harvard Business Review*, 91.3 (2013), 117–20, 135. PMID: 23451530.

Brian Cox: Focus On What You Don't Know

1   Mark R. Leary, Kate J. Diebels, Erin K. Davisson, Katrina P. Jongman-Sereno, Jennifer C. Isherwood, Kaitlin T. Raimi, Samantha A. Deffler and Rick H. Hoyle, 'Cognitive and Interpersonal Features of Intellectual Humility', *Personality and Social Psychology Bulletin* (March 2017). doi.org/10.1177/0146167217697695.

2   Amy Y. Ou, David A. Waldman and Suzanne J. Peterson, 'Do Humble CEOs Matter? An Examination of CEO Humility and Firm Outcomes', *Journal of Management* 44.3 (2018), 1147–73. This research was also cited in this article: 'Leaders are More Powerful When They're Humble, New Research Shows', *The Washington Post*. Published online 8 December 2016.

Barry Hearn: What Story Are You Telling Yourself?

1   Fritz Heider, *The Life of a Psychologist: An Autobiography* (University Press of Kansas, 1983).

2   Fritz Heider and Marianne Simmel, 'An Experimental Study of Apparent Behavior', *The American Journal of Psychology* 57.2 (1944), 243–59. Also cited here: 'The

Psychology of Stories: The Storytelling Formula Our Brains Crave', Hubspot.com.

3   I. DeWitt, J. P. Rauschecker, 'Wernicke's Area Revisited: Parallel Streams and Word Processing', *BrainLang*, 127.2 (2013), 181–91.

Shane Parrish: Show Me Your Calendar

1   Shane Parrish, *Clear Thinking: Turning Ordinary Moments into Extraordinary Results* (Portfolio/Penguin, 2023).

2   'Doing Unto Future Selves As You Would Do Unto Others: Psychological Distance and Decision Making', SemanticScholar.org.

Usain Bolt: Transform Your Mindset

1   M. P. Muehlenbein and D. P. Watts, 'The Costs of Dominance: Testosterone, Cortisol and Intestinal Parasites In Wild Male Chimpanzees', *BioPsychoSocial Medicine*, 4.21 (December 2010). doi.org/10.1186/1751-0759-4-21. PMID: 21143892; PMCID: PMC3004803.

Elizabeth A. Tibbetts, Juanita Pardo-Sanchez and Chloe Weise, 'The Establishment and Maintenance of Dominance Hierarchies', *Philosophical Transactions of the Royal Society B* (2022), B37720200450.

2   Shawn N. Geniole, Brian M. Bird, Erika L. Ruddick, Justin M. Carré, 'Effects of Competition Outcome on Testosterone Concentrations in Humans: An Updated Meta-Analysis', *Hormones and Behavior*, 92 (2017), 37–50.

3   Steve Magness, *Do Hard Things: Why We Get Resilience Wrong and the Surprising Science of Real Toughness* (HarperOne, 2022). I also referenced Will Storr, *The Status*

Game: On Human Life and How to Play It (William Collins, 2022).

4   Carol Dweck, *Mindset: How You Can Fulfil Your Potential* (Robinson, 2012).

Tom Daley: Process Goals Beat Outcome Goals

1   A. M. Freund and M. Hennecke, 'Changing Eating Behaviour vs. Losing Weight: The Role of Goal Focus for Weight Loss in Overweight Women', *Psychology & Health*, 27.2 (2012), 25–42. doi.org/10.1080/08870446.2011.570867.

2   Edwin A. Locke and Gary P. Latham, 'Building a Practically Useful Theory of Goal Setting and Task Motivation: A 35-Year Odyssey', *American Psychologist*, 57.9 (2002), 705.

Sabrina Cohen-Hatton: Three Questions for Better Decisions

1   J. E. Raymond, J. L. O'Brien, 'Selective Visual Attention and Motivation: The Consequences of Value Learning in an Attentional Blink Task', *Psychological Science*, 20.8 (2009), 981–8. doi.org/10.1111/j.1467-9280.2009.02391.x.

Charles Duhigg: Hug, Hear or Help?

1   G. J. Stephens, L. J. Silbert, U. Hasson, 'Speaker–Listener Neural Coupling Underlies Successful Communication', *Proceedings of the National Academy of Sciences of the USA*, 107.32 (2010), 14425–30. doi.org/10.1073/pnas.1008662107.

NOTES

AJ Tracey: The Power of Your Inner Circle

1. Nicholas A. Christakis and James H. Fowler, 'The Spread of Obesity in a Large Social Network Over 32 Years', *New England Journal of Medicine*, 357.4 (2007), 370–79.

2. K. Desender, S. Beurms and E. Van den Bussche, 'Is Mental Effort Exertion Contagious?', *Psychonomic Bulletin & Review*, 23 (2016), 624–31.

George Russell: Ask for Help

1. Heidi Grant, *Reinforcements: How to Get People to Help You* (Harvard Business Press, 2018).

2. D. T. Miller, 'The Norm of Self-Interest', *American Psychologist*, 54.12 (1999), 1053–60. doi.org/10.1037/0003-066X.54.12.1053.

3. Oliver Scott Curry, Lee A. Rowland, Caspar J. Van Lissa, Sally Zlotowitz, John McAlaney, Harvey Whitehouse, 'Happy to Help? A Systematic Review and Meta-Analysis of the Effects of Performing Acts of Kindness on the Well-Being of the Actor', *Journal of Experimental Social Psychology*, 76 (2018), 320–29. doi.org/10.1016/j.jesp.2018.02.014.

4. A. W. Brooks, F. Gino and M. E. Schweitzer, 'Smart People Ask For (My) Advice: Seeking Advice Boosts Perceptions of Competence', *Management Science*, 61.6 (2015), 1421–35. doi.org/10.1287/mnsc.2014.2054.

Dan Carter: How to Read Emotions

1. Dr Ceri Evans, *Perform Under Pressure: Change the Way You Feel, Think and Act Under Pressure* (Thorsons, 2019).

NOTES

Marcus Wareing: Surround Yourself with the Best

1. 'Imitation Is Inspiration', PsychologyToday.com. Published online 17 October 2022.
2. Katie S. Mehr, Amanda E. Geiser, Katherine L. Milkman and Angela L. Duckworth, 'Copy-Paste Prompts: A New Nudge to Promote Goal Achievement', *Journal of the Association for Consumer Research*, 5.3. First published online 11 May 2020. doi.org/10.1086/708880.

   Samuli Reijula and Ralph Hertwig, 'Self-Nudging and the Citizen Choice Architect', *Behavioural Public Policy*. First published online 26 March 2020. doi.org/10.1017/bpp.2020.5.

Sir Ian McGeechan: Always Shout Your Round

1. A. Simms, T. Nichols, 'Social Loafing: A Review of the Literature', *Journal of Management Policy and Practice*, 15.1 (2014), 58–67.
2. Stephen G. Harkins and Jeffrey M. Jackson, 'The Role of Evaluation in Eliminating Social Loafing', *Personality and Social Psychology Bulletin*, 11.4 (1985), 457–65.

Kevin Sinfield: The Helping Hand

1. R. E. Ingram, 'Self-Focused Attention in Clinical Disorders: Review and a Conceptual Model', *Psychological Bulletin*, 107 (1990), 156–76.
2. E. W. Dunn, L. B. Aknin and M. I. Norton, 'Spending Money on Others Promotes Happiness', *Science*, 319.5870 (2008), 1687–88.

NOTES

3   S. Park, T. Kahnt, A. Dogan, et al., 'A Neural Link Between Generosity and Happiness', *Nature Communications*, 8.15964 (2017). doi.org/10.1038/ncomms15964.

4   Y. J. Wong, M. Shea, S-Y. Wang and J. Cheng, 'The Encouragement Character Strength Scale: Scale Development and Psychometric Properties', *Journal of Counseling Psychology*, 66.3 (2019), 362–74. doi.org/10.1037/cou0000334.

5   Marianna Pogosyan, 'In Helping Others, You Help Yourself', PsychologyToday.com. Published online 30 May 2018.

Susan Krauss Whitbourne, '12 Ways to Find Out If You're the Kind of Person Others Like', PsychologyToday.com. Published online 27 April 2019.

Martin Lewis: Trust Comes First

1   '19th Annual Global CEO Survey: Redefining Business Success in a Changing World', Pwc.com.

2   Ana Cristina Costa, Ashley Fulmer, Neil Anderson, 'Trust in Work Teams: An Integrative Review, Multilevel Framework, and Future Directions', *Journal of Organizational Behavior*, 39.2 (2017). doi.org/10.1002/job.2213.

3   Heather Harper, 'How to Build Trust in Teams', WorkStyle.io. Updated 14 March 2023.

4   A. C. Costa, R. A. Roe, T. Taillieu, 'Trust Within Teams: The Relation with Performance Effectiveness', *European Journal of Work and Organizational Psychology*, 10.3 (2001), 225–44. doi.org/10.1080/13594320143000654.

5   A. C. Costa, 'Work Team Trust and Effectiveness', *Personnel Review*, 32.5 (2003), 605–22. doi.org/10.1108/00483480310488360.

6   Ron Friedman, *The Best Place to Work: The Art and Science of Creating an Extraordinary Workplace* (Perigee, 2015).

7   Eric M. VanEpps, Einav Hart and Maurice Schweitzer, 'How to Self-Promote – Without Sounding Self-Centered', *Harvard Business Review*. Published online 20 November 2023.

Andy Cole: 'We' Not 'Me'

1   R. B. Cialdini, R. J. Borden, A. Thorne, M. R. Walker, S. Freeman and L. R. Sloan, 'Basking in Reflected Glory: Three (Football) Field Studies', *Journal of Personality and Social Psychology*, 34.3 (1976), 366–75. doi.org/10.1037/0022-3514.34.3.366.

M. L. Newman, J. W. Pennebaker, D. S. Berry, J. M. Richards, 'Lying Words: Predicting Deception From Linguistic Styles', *Personality & Social Psychology Bulletin*, 29.5 (2003), 665–75.

2   Ariana Orvell, Ethan Kross, Susan A. Gelman, 'How "You" Makes Meaning', *Science* (March 2017), 1299–1302.

3   Susan Gelman, 'How Saying "Me" or "We" Changes Your Psychological Response', BigThink.com. Published online 31 March 2023.

Chris Voss: Small Talk Gets Big Wins

1   N. Bose, D. Sgroi, 'The Role of Personality Beliefs and "Small Talk" in Strategic Behaviour', *PLOS One*, 17.9 (2022), e0269523. doi.org/10.1371/journal.pone.0269523.

Joe Marler: Emotional Glue

1   S. A. Haslam, S. D. Reicher, M. J. Platow, *The New Psychology of Leadership: Identity, Influence and Power* (2nd ed.) (Routledge, 2020).

NOTES

2. S. G. Barsade and O. A. O'Neill, 'What's Love Got to Do With It? A Longitudinal Study of the Culture of Companionate Love and Employee and Client Outcomes in a Long-term Care Setting', *Administrative Science Quarterly*, 59.4 (2014), 551–598. doi.org/10.1177/0001839214538636.

Pippa Grange: The Triple H

1. It is often credited to the author Jon Gordon, who wrote a popular book with Mike Smith: *You Win in the Locker Room First: 7C's to Build a Winning Team in Sports, Business, and Life* (Wiley, 2015).
2. Konrad Marshall, *Yellow & Black: A Season with Richmond* (Slattery Media Group, 2018).
3. Personal stories from this session are also found here: www.smh.com.au/interactive/2017/brandon-ellis/
4. Dr Pippa Grange, *Fear Less: How to Win at Life Without Losing Yourself* (Vermillion, 2020).

Sara Davies: Radical Candour

1. Kim Scott, *Radical Candor: How to Get What You Want by Saying What You Mean* (Pan Books, 2019).
2. Carlton Fong, Diane Schallert, Kyle Williams, Zachary Williamson, Shengjie Lin, Young Won Kim, Ling-Hui Chen, 'Making Feedback Constructive: The Interplay of Undergraduates' Motivation with Perceptions of Feedback Specificity and Friendliness', *Educational Psychology*, 41 (2021).
3. Denise McLain and Bailey Nelson, 'How Effective Feedback Fuels Performance', Gallup.com. Updated 19 January 2024.

NOTES

Jordan Henderson: Dealing with Dissenters

1. Phil Daoust, 'Office Too Hot? Computer Playing Up? Go on, Have a Grumble, it's Good for You', *Guardian*, 4 September 2017.

2. 'The Cult of Complaining: Why do we Spend so Much Time Moaning About Work?', Stylist.co.uk.

3. Joanna Wolfe and Elizabeth Powell, 'Gender and Expressions of Dissatisfaction: A Study of Complaining in Mixed-Gendered Student Work Groups', *Women & Language*, 29.2 (2006), 13. www.researchgate.net/publication/283057231.

4. This quote was found in numerous places: 'Moaning is Bad for Your Health', *The Irish Times*, and 'Use This Harvard Researcher's Stoic Test to Quit Complaining and Be Happier,' Inc.com.

5. R. T. Waska, 'Projective Identification, Countertransference, and the Struggle for Understanding Over Acting Out', *Journal of Psychotherapy Practice and Research*, 8.2 (1999), 155–61.

6. P. Niedenthal, L. Barsalou, P. Winkelman, et al., 'Embodiment in Attitudes, Social Perception, and Emotion', *Personality and Social Psychology Reviews*, 9 (2005), 184–211.

Gordon Ramsay: Don't Take It So Personally

1. Avraham Kluger, Angelo DeNisi, 'The Effects of Feedback Interventions on Performance: A Historical Review, a Meta-Analysis, and a Preliminary Feedback Intervention Theory', *Psychological Bulletin*, 119 (1996), 254–84. doi.org/10.1037/0033-2909.119.2.254.

2. Marie-Hélène Budworth, Gary Latham, Laxmikant Manroop, 'Looking Forward to Performance Improvement: A Field Test of the Feedforward Interview for Performance

Management', *Human Resource Management*, 54 (2014). doi.org/10.1002/hrm.21618.

Dame Laura Kenny: Disagree Agreeably

1   'The Difficult Conversations Lab', Research Projects, Columbia Climate School.

   K. G. Kugler and P. T. Coleman, 'Get Complicated: The Effects of Complexity on Conversations Over Potentially Intractable Moral Conflicts', *Negotiation and Conflict Management Research*, 13.3 (2020), 211–30. doi.org/10.1111/ncmr.12192.

   Anna Antinori, Olivia L. Carter, Luke D. Smillie, 'Seeing it Both Ways: Openness to Experience and Binocular Rivalry Suppression', *Journal of Research in Personality*, 68 (2017), 15–22. doi.org/10.1016/j.jrp.2017.03.005.

Steve Peters: 'What if . . . ?'

1   Chris Hoy, *HP* interview; Steve Peters, *The Chimp Paradox* (Vermilion, 2012).

2   Gary A. Klein, *The Power of Intuition: How to Use Your Gut Feelings to Make Better Decisions at Work* (Crown Currency, 2004).

   Gary A. Klein, *Sources of Power: How People Make Decisions* (MIT Press, 1998).

3   D. J. Mitchell, J. E. Russo and N. Pennington, 'Back to the Future: Temporal Perspective in the Explanation of Events', *Journal of Behavioral Decision Making*, 2.1 (1989), 25–38. doi.org/10.1002/bdm.3960020103.

NOTES

Alex Honnold: Embrace the Fear

1   A. Pittig, M. Treanor, R. T. LeBeau, M. G. Craske, 'The Role of Associative Fear and Avoidance Learning in Anxiety Disorders: Gaps and Directions for Future Research', *Neuroscience & Biobehavioral Review*, 88 (2018), 117–40. doi.org/10.1016/j.neubiorev.2018.03.015.

2   V. Meyer, 'Modification of Expectations in Cases with Obsessional Rituals', *Behaviour Research and Therapy*, 4 (1966), 273–80.

3   P. Siegel and B. S. Peterson, '"All we Have to Fear is Fear Itself": Paradigms for Reducing Fear by Preventing Awareness of It', *Psychological Bulletin*, 150.9 (2024), 1118–54.

Graham Potter: No Comfort Zones

1   This quote was taken from an interview in *The Athletic*: '"Genius" Graham Potter's Remarkable Road to Premier League Coaching.' Published 7 September 2022.

2   T. Senninger, *Abenteuer Leiten – in Abenteuern Lernen* (Ökotopia Verlag, 2000).

Maro Itoje: The Shit People Don't See

1   R. F. Baumeister, D. G. Hutton and K. J. Cairns, 'Negative Effects of Praise on Skilled Performance', *Basic and Applied Social Psychology*, 11.2 (1990), 131–48.

James Milner: The Commitment Principle

1   N. J. Allen and J. P. Meyer, 'The Measurement and Antecedents of Affective, Continuance and Normative

NOTES

Commitment to the Organization', *Journal of Occupational Psychology*, 63.1 (1990), 1–18. doi.org/10.1111/j.2044-8325.1990.tb00506.x.

J. P. Meyer and N. J. Allen, 'A Three Component Conceptualization of Organizational Commitment', *Human Resource Management Review* (April 2002).

2. S. Grimsley and J. Allison, 'Organizational Commitment: Definition, Theory & Types', (October 2015). study.com/academy/lesson/organizational-commitment-definition-theory-types.html.

   G. V. Prabhakar and P. Ram, 'Antecedent HRM Practices for Organizational Commitment', *International Journal of Business and Social Science*, 2.2 (2011), 55–62. ijbssnet.com/journals/Vol._2_No._2%3B_February_2011/6.pdf

3. S. Grimsley and J. Allison, 'Organizational Commitment: Definition, Theory & Types'.

   'Porter and Lawler Model of Motivation (with Diagram)'. yourarticlelibrary.com/entrepreneurship/motivation-entrepreneurship/porter-and-lawler-model-of-motivation-with-diagram/53299.

   R. M. Steers, 'When is an Organization Effective? A Process Approach to Understanding Effectiveness', *Organizational Dynamics*, 5.2 (1976), 50–63. doi.org/10.1016/0090-2616(76)90054-1.

4. 'What is Affective Commitment?', Organizational Psychology Degrees (1 July 2019). organizationalpsychologydegrees.com/faq/what-is-affective-commitment/

5. A. Cohen, 'Commitment Before and After: An Evaluation and Reconceptualization of Organizational Commitment', *Human Resource Management Review*, 17.3 (2007), 336–354. doi.org/10.1016/j.hrmr.2007.05.001.

   'Affective Commitment', TheDecisionLab.com.

NOTES

Alun Wyn Jones: The IKEA Effect

1. M. I. Norton, D. Mochon, D. Ariely, 'The IKEA Effect: When Labor Leads to Love', *Journal of Consumer Psychology*, 22.3 (2012), 453–60. doi.org/10.1016/j.jcps.2011.08.002.

   L. E. Marsh, P. Kanngiesser, B. Hood, 'When and How does Labour Lead to Love? The Ontogeny and Mechanisms of the IKEA Effect', *Cognition*, 170 (2018), 245–53. doi.org/10.1016/j.cognition.2017.10.012.

Steven Gerrard: All In

1. Steven Gerrard and Henry Winter, *Gerrard: My Autobiography* (Bantam, 2007).
2. Peter Richmond, *Phil Jackson: Lord of the Rings* (Penguin, 2013).
3. G. B. Samdal, et al., 'Effective Behaviour Change Techniques for Physical Activity and Healthy Eating in Overweight and Obese Adults; Systematic Review and Meta-Regression Analyses', *International Journal of Behavioral Nutrition and Physical Activity*. Full Text at biomedcentral.com.
4. R. B. Cialdini, *Influence: The Psychology of Persuasion* (Harper Collins, 2007).

Joe Wicks: Retire Every Year

1. A. Rees, M. W. Wiggins, W. S. Helton, T. Loveday, D. O'Hare, 'The Impact of Breaks on Sustained Attention in a Simulated, Semi-Automated Train Control Task', *Applied Cognitive Psychology*, 31.3 (2017), 351–59. doi.org/10.1002/acp.3334. First cited here: https://www.apa.org/monitor/2019/01/break.

2   Ibid.

3   Hans Henrik Sievertsen, Francesca Gino and Marco Piovesan, 'Cognitive Fatigue Influences Students' Performance on Standardized Tests', *Proceedings of the National Academy of Sciences*, 113.10 (2016), 2621–24.

4   Tim Ferriss, *The 4-Hour Workweek: Escape 9–5, Live Anywhere, and Join the New Rich* (Harmony Books, 2009).

Vicky Pattison: Number Your Days

1   A. Gragnano, S. Simbula, M. Miglioretti, 'Work–Life Balance: Weighing the Importance of Work–Family and Work–Health Balance', *International Journal of Environmental Research and Public Health*, 17.3 (2020), 907. doi.org/10.3390/ijerph17030907.

2   Frank Pega, et al., 'Global, Regional, and National Burdens of Ischemic Heart Disease and Stroke Attributable to Exposure to Long Working Hours for 194 Countries, 2000–2016: A Systematic Analysis from the WHO/ILO Joint Estimates of the Work-Related Burden of Disease and Injury', *Environment International*, 154 (2021), 106595.

3   B. Hruska, S. D. Pressman, K. Bendinskas, B. B. Gump, 'Do Vacations Alter the Connection Between Stress and Cardiovascular Activity? The Effects of a Planned Vacation on the Relationship Between Weekly Stress and Ambulatory Heart Rate', *Pyschology & Health*, 35 (2020), 984–99. doi.org/10.1080/08870446.2019.1687699.

4   Larissa Bolliger, et al., 'The Association Between Day-To-Day Stress Experiences, Recovery, and Work Engagement Among Office Workers in Academia–An Ecological Momentary Assessment Study', *PLOS One*, 18.2 (2023). doi.org/10.1371/journal.pone.0281556.

J. de Bloom, S. A. Geurts, M. A. Kompier, 'Effects of Short Vacations, Vacation Activities and Experiences On Employee Health and Well-Being', *Stress & Health*, 28.4 (2012), 305–18. doi.org/10.1002/smi.1434.

Eddie Howe: Reflect to Reconnect

1 S. Sonnentag and C. Fritz, 'The Recovery Experience Questionnaire: Development and Validation of a Measure for Assessing Recuperation and Unwinding from Work', *Journal of Occupational Health Psychology*, 12.3 (2007), 204–21. doi.org/10.1037/1076-8998.12.3.204.

2 O. B. Davidson, et al., 'Sabbatical Leave: Who Gains and How Much?', *Journal of Applied Psychology*, 95.5 (2010), 953–64. doi.org/10.1037/a0020068. PMID: 20718526.

3 'Eddie Howe hopes his cultural reboot of Newcastle will reap rewards at Spurs', *Guardian*, 2 April 2022. https://www.theguardian.com/football/2022/apr/02/eddie-howe-hopes-his-cultural-reboot-of-newcastle-will-reap-rewards-at-spurs

4 Ibid.

Emily Maitlis: Golden Time

1 I. Kirste, Z. Nicola, G. Kronenberg, T. L. Walker, R. C. Liu, G. Kempermann, 'Is Silence Golden? Effects of Auditory Stimuli and Their Absence on Adult Hippocampal Neurogenesis', *Brain Structure and Function*, 220.2 (2015), 1221–28. doi.org/10.1007/s00429-013-0679-3. Also cited here: 'The Power of Silence', ThePositivePsychologyPeople.com.

2 B. Ainsworth, H. Bolderston, M. Garner, 'Testing the Differential Effects of Acceptance and Attention-Based

Psychological Interventions on Intrusive Thoughts and Worry', *Behaviour Research and Therapy*, 91 (2017), 72–77. Also cited here: 'Testing the Differential Effects of Acceptance and Attention-Based Psychological Interventions on Intrusive Thoughts and Worry,' ScienceDirect.com.

James Timpson: Celebrate the Good News First

1 Nathaniel Lambert, A. Marlea Gwinn, et al., 'A Boost of Positive Affect the Perks of Sharing Positive Experiences', *Journal of Social and Personal Relationships*, 30 (2013), 24–43. doi.org/10.1177/0265407512449400.

Sarina Wiegman: Attitude: Gratitude

1 R. W. L. Lau, S. T. Cheng, 'Gratitude Lessens Death Anxiety', *European Journal of Ageing*, 8.3 (2011), 169. doi.org/10.1007/s10433-011-0195-3.

Sara Pascoe: Unconditional Positive Regard

1 C. R. Rogers, 'Significant Aspects of Client-Centered Therapy', *American Psychologist*, 1.10 (1946), 415–22. doi.org/10.1037/h0060866.
C. R. Rogers, *Client-Centered Therapy: Its Current Practice, Implications and Theory* (Constable, 1951).
C. R. Rogers. 'The Necessary and Sufficient Conditions of Therapeutic Personality Change', *Journal of Consulting Psychology*, 21 (1957), 95–103. doi.org/10.1037/h0045357.
C. R. Rogers, 'Therapy, Personality and Interpersonal Relationships', in S. Koch (Ed.), *Psychology: A Study of a Science, Formulations of the Person and the Social Context* (McGraw-Hill, 1959).

NOTES

C. R. Rogers, 'Client-Centered/Person-Centered Approach to Therapy', *Voprosy Psikhologii*, 2 (2001), 48–58.

2   Lauren Kelly McHenry, 'A Qualitative Exploration of Unconditional Positive Regard and its Opposite Constructs in Coach-Athlete Relationships' (2018). Cited in Nir Eyal, 'The Surprising Benefits of Unconditional Positive Regard', Medium, 18 July 2020. medium.com/behavior-design/the-surprising-benefits-of-unconditional-positive-regard-973cb9d9baa7.

3   Evi Makri-Botsari, 'Adolescents' Unconditional Acceptance by Parents and Teachers and Educational Outcomes: A Structural Model of Gender Differences', *Journal of Adolescence*, 43 (2015), 50–62.

Jason Fox: What Would a Commando Do?

1   'This simple strategy teaches kids not to give up', *Psychology Today*. www.psychologytoday.com/us/blog/what-mentally-strong-people-dont-do/201802/how-use-the-batman-effect-teach-kids-perseverance. The study cited is R. E. White and S. M. Carlson, 'What Would Batman Do? Self-Distancing Improves Executive Function in Young Children', *Developmental Science*, 19.3 (2016), 1–8.

2   Ibid. See also 'The "Batman Effect": How Having an Alter Ego Empowers You', U-M LSA Department of Psychology (umich.edu).

INDEX

Abdaal, Ali, 49–52
Ali, Muhammad, 217
All Blacks, 115–19
Allen, Natalie, 200–202
Almirón, Miguel, 224
Alonso, Fernando, 182–4
Amabile, Teresa, 95
American football, 154
amygdala, 186
Andrew, Duke of York, 226–8
antidepressants, 41
anxiety, 55
appreciation, expression of, 10
Ariely, Dan, 205
Armstrong, Lance, 145–6
assurance, 62
Atlanta Falcons, 154
Atomic Habits (Clear), 8
Attia, Peter, 7–8
Auschwitz concentration
    camp, 46
Australian-rules football, 154–5
autism, 48

Baumeister, Roy, 196
Bennett, Alan, 10
BIRG effect, 143

Boehly, Todd, 190
Bolt, Usain, 10, 85–91
Bournemouth AFC, 221
brain, 54, 99, 166
    amygdala, 186
    chimp brain, 177–81
    cognitive depletion, 214–15
    generosity and, 132
    storytelling and, 78, 104
British & Irish Lions, 4, 126,
    203, 206
Broad, Stuart, 64–6
Burrow, Rob, 130

calendars, 82–4
calling, work as, 17–19
Cambodia, 41–4
Cameron, David, 134
Carter, Dan, 115–19
chimp brain, 177–81
Cialdini, Robert, 142, 210
cleaning, 18
Clear, James, 8
Clear Thinking (Parrish), 81
cognitive depletion, 214–15
Cohen-Hatton, Sabrina, 97–100
Cole, Andy, 141–4

INDEX

Columbia University, 132
comfort zone, 189–92
commando spirit, 242–6
commitment, 199–202
communication, 103–6
companionate love, 152
complaints, 164–7
concentration camps, 46
Concorde, 47
connections, 101–19
   asking for help, 111–14
   communication, 103–6
   emotional literacy, 115–19
   inner circle, 107–10
consistency, 5, 9, 87–8
CORF effect, 143
Covid-19 pandemic (2019–23), 24, 213
Cox, Brian, 70–73
Crafter's Companion, 159
cricket, 64–9
cycling, 171–4, 177–81

Dachau concentration camp, 46
Daley, Tom, 92–6
Dallas Buyers Club (2013 film), 34, 35–6
Davies, Sara, 159–63
Davis, Steve, 75
Deci, Edward, 28–30
decisions, 97–100
defeat, 85–91
delayed gratification, 10, 34–8
depression, 41–4, 55
Detachment-Recovery Model, 222

Dragon's Den, 159
Duckworth, Angela, 125
Duhigg, Charles, 103–6
Duke University, 71, 228
Dweck, Carol, 89–90

efficiency, 61
effortful tasks, 197
El Capitan, California, 185–6
Eleven Madison Park, New York, 59
emotions
   chimp brain and, 177–81
   drivers, 149–52
   game face, 182–4
   literacy, 115–19
empathy, 62
England national cricket team, 64–9
England national football team
   men's, 153, 156
   women's, 10, 234–6
England Rugby League, 1–3, 5
England Rugby Union, 4, 149–52
Epstein, Jeffrey, 226–8
eulogies, 35, 50–52
Evans, Ceri, 116
exercise, 8, 51
exposure therapy, 186
extrinsic motivation, 27–33
Eyal, Nir, 240

failure, 85–91
Farnam Street, 81–2

INDEX

Federal Bureau of Investigation (FBI), 145–8
feedback, 157–74
   complaints, 164–7
   criticism, 168–70
   radical candour, 159–63
Feel-Good Productivity (Abdaal), 50
Ferguson, Alex, 141
Ferriss, Tim, 215
Filofax, 5
fire service, 97–100
fixed mindset, 89–90
focus, 57–78
   humility and, 70–73
   presence, 61
   priorities, 82–4
   promotion vs prevention, 67–9
   seriousness, 61
   storytelling, 74–8
Formula One, 15, 111–14, 182–4
Fox, Jason, 242–6
Framingham Heart Study, 109
Frankl, Viktor, 46–7
Fraser, Henry, 150
Freedman, Dougie, 9
Freelance Programmers, 47
Friedman, Ron, 137
friendships, 53–5
Fritz, Charlotte, 222

game face, 182–4
Gelman, Susan, 143
Geordie Shore, 217
George Mason University, 214
Gerrard, Steven, 208–10
goals, 92–6
good news, 231–3
Grange, Pippa, 153–6
gratitude, 234–6
Grit (Duckworth), 125
growth mindset, 89–90
Guidara, Will, 59–63

habits, 8–9
Halvorson, Heidi Grant, 67
Hari, Johann, 41–2
Harlequins FC, 149–52
Hearn, Barry, 74–8
Heider, Fritz, 77
helping others, 130–33
Helton, William, 214
Henderson, Jordan, 164–7, 177
Higgins, Edward Tory, 67
Hill, Patrick, 43
Hodgkinson, Keely, 26–33
Holocaust (1941–5), 46
Homer, 21
Honnold, Alex, 185–8
hostage negotiation, 145–8
Howe, Eddie, 221–5
Hoy, Chris, 177
humility, 70–73

identity, 151
IKEA effect, 205–7
Influence (Cialdini), 210
inner circle, 107–10
intrinsic motivation, 28–33
Itoje, Maro, 195–8

INDEX

Jackson, Phil, 209
job crafting, 18
Joelinton, 224
Jones, Eddie, 4

Kane, Aldo, 244
Kenny, Laura, 171–4
Kidd, Brian, 141–2
Kirste, Imke, 228
Klein, Gary, 180
Klein, Melanie, 166
Klopp, Jürgen, 164–7, 199–202
Kluger, Avraham, 170
Kramer, Steven, 95
Kross, Ethan, 143, 245–6

Lally, Phillippa, 8
Le Gavroche, London, 124–5, 169
Learning Zone Model, 191
Leeds Rhinos, 2, 130
Lewis, Martin, 134–6
life expectancy, 8
Liverpool FC, 164–7, 199–202, 208–10
Livingstone, Tim, 155
Lohr, Jeffrey, 166
Lost Connections (Hari), 42

Magness, Steve, 89
Maitlis, Emily, 226–8
Manchester United FC, 141–4
Marler, Joe, 149–52
Marshall, Mel, 21
marshmallow test, 36–8
Martinenghi, Nicolò, 23

Matchroom, 75
McConaughey, Matthew, 10, 34–8
McCullum, Brendon, 65–9
McCurry, Shane, 154
McGeechan, Ian, 4–6, 126–9
Mental Analysis and Development Group, 116
Meyer, John, 200–202
Meyer, Victor, 187
Michigan State University, 165
Miller, Dale, 113
Mills, Glen, 86–7
Milner, James, 199–202
mindset, 7
    aggressive, 64–9
    emotional literacy and, 116–17
    gladiatorial, 20
    growth, 89–90
    scientific, 70–73
    work orientation, 18–19
Mischel, Walter, 36–8
moaning, 164–7
Mochon, Daniel, 205
monomania, 16–17
morning alarms, 3–4
mortality, 35, 50–52
motivation, 13–38
    delayed gratification, 10, 34–8
    intrinsic vs extrinsic, 27–33
    Odysseus contracts, 21–5, 26
    promotion vs prevention, 67–9
    self-determination theory, 30

visualisation, 31–2, 92–3
work orientations, 17–19
motor neurone disease (MND), 130

National Gallery, London, 10
neocortex, 178
New Zealand national rugby team, 115–19
Newcastle United FC, 141, 142, 222–5
Nir, Dina, 170
Norris, Lando, 15–19
Norton, Michael, 205
numbering days, 217–20

O'Neill, Rob, 5, 7
obituaries, 50
Odysseus contracts, 21–5, 26
Olympic Games, 20–25, 92, 171
  2004 Athens, 86, 92
  2008 Beijing, 88
  2012 London, 92–6
  2016 Rio, 172
  2021 Tokyo, 20, 30, 32
  2024 Paris, 21, 30–31, 33
optimism, 229–46
  commando spirit, 242–6
  good news, 231–3
  gratitude, 234–6
  unconditional positive regard, 237–41
organisation, 79–100
  decisions, 97–100
  failure and, 85–91

priorities, 82–4
process goals, 92–6
Orvell, Ariana, 143

Parrish, Shane, 81–4
Parrish, Steve, 9
Pascoe, Sara, 237–41
Pattison, Vicky, 217–20
Peacock, Jamie, 1–3
Peaty, Adam, 20–25
Peters, Steve, 172, 177–81
Phelps, Michael, 23, 183
Potter, Graham, 189–92
power pose, 183
pre-mortems, 181
presence, 61
pressure, 5, 151, 175–92
  chimp brain and, 177–81
  comfort zone and, 189–92
  decisions and, 97–100
  emotional literacy and, 115–19
  exposure therapy and, 185–8
prevention focus, 67–9
priorities, 82–4
pro-social conduct, 130–33
process goals, 92–6
Progress Principle, The (Amabile and Kramer), 95
promotion focus, 67–9
purpose, 38–52
  mortality and, 50–52
  why, 53–5

Radical Candor (Scott), 160, 162
Ramsay, Gordon, 168–70

reflection, 221–5
reliability, 62
responsiveness, 62
rest, 211–28
    golden time, 226–8
    mini-retirements, 213–16
    numbering days, 217–20
    reflection and, 221–5
retirement, 213–16
Richesin, Matthew, 183
Richmond Tigers, 154–5
Ringelmann, Max, 128
Robbins, Mel, 7
Rogers, Carl, 238–9
Rohn, Jim, 110
Ronaldo, Cristiano, 183
Roux, Albert, 124, 169
Russell, George, 111–14
Ryan, Richard, 28–30

sacrifice, 22
Saracens, 195–8
Savoy, Guy, 169
Scott, Jill, 234–5
Scott, Kim, 160, 162
self-determination theory, 30
self-esteem, 237–41
Senninger, Tom, 191
seriousness, 61
sexism, 47
shared identity, 151
Shirley, Stephanie, 45–8
Simmel, Marianne, 77
Sinek, Simon, 53–5
Sinfield, Kevin, 130–33
small talk, 145–8

Smith, Mike, 154
Smith, Tony, 1
social identity theory, 151
social loafing, 128–9
Sonnentag, Sabine, 222
Southgate, Gareth 156
Stanford University, 89, 113
Stokes, Ben, 64
storytelling, 74–8, 104
Summerfield, Derek, 41
Supercommunicators
    (Duhigg), 103
Swan Lake (Tchaikovsky),
    190–91
swimming, 20–25, 92–6

tangibles, 62
teams, 121–56
    copying, 123–5
    emotional drivers, 149–52
    emotional literacy and,
        115–19
    pro-social conduct,
        130–33
    shared identity, 151
    small talk, 145–8
    social loafing, 128–9
    Triple H exercise, 154–6
    trust, 134–8
    'we' not 'me', 141–4
Timpson, James, 231–3
Tomkins, Sam, 5
Tracey, AJ, 107–10
Triple H exercise, 154–6
Trippier, Kieran, 224
trust, 134–8

truth, 75
TSPDS, 195–8

unconditional positive regard, 239
United States Navy SEALs, 5
University College London, 8
University of Arkansas, 166
University of Michigan, 245–6
University of Rochester, 28, 43
University of Tennessee, 183
University of Warwick, 146

visualisation, 31–2, 92–3
Voss, Chris, 145–8

Wane, Shaun, 5–6, 11
Wareing, Marcus, 123–5
'we' not 'me', 141–4
Wernicke's area, 78
What if?, 179–81
White, Marco Pierre, 169

Wicks, Joe, 213–16
Wiegman, Sarina, 10, 234–6
Winfrey, Oprah, 145–6
Wolff, Toto, 112–13
work, 193–210
  commitment, 199–202, 208–10
  IKEA effect, 205–7
  TSPDS, 195–8
work orientations, 17–19
World Health Organization (WHO), 42–3
Wrzesniewski, Amy, 16–18
Wyn Jones, Alun, 203–7

Yale School of Management, 16
Yale University, 173
Yellow & Black (Hardwick and Marshall), 155

Zak, Paul, 77

ABOUT THE AUTHORS

Jake Humphrey is one of Britain's best-respected sports presenters. Formerly lead Premier League presenter at BT Sport, Jake has covered events ranging from Formula 1 to the London Olympics and was the youngest-ever presenter of the BBC's *Match of the Day*.

Damian Hughes is an expert on high-performing cultures. A trusted advisor to businesses and sportspeople around the world, he has been praised by the likes of Richard Branson, Muhammad Ali, Roger Bannister and Alex Ferguson. He has been a visiting professor at Manchester Metropolitan University and his work has been translated into ten languages.

Jake and Damian are the creators of *High Performance*, the UK's most-downloaded podcast on the psychology of success. In just five years, they have interviewed unicorn-founding CEOs and World Heavyweight Champion boxers, completed two sell-out tours, and published three bestselling books about the psychology of success.